Anthropology
of Addictions
and Recovery

Tobacco, a New World plant, was observed by Europeans to be a part of healing ceremonies performed by Native American shamans, as depicted here.

Anthropology of Addictions and Recovery

Irene Glasser

Center for Alcohol and Addiction Studies
Brown University

WAVELAND

PRESS, INC.

Long Grove, Illinois

For information about this book, contact:
  Waveland Press, Inc.
  4180 IL Route 83, Suite 101
  Long Grove, IL 60047-9580
  (847) 634-0081
  info@waveland.com
  www.waveland.com

Photo credits: ii Courtesy of the John Carter Brown Library at Brown University. **34** Courtesy of the Charles Deering McCormick Library of Special Collections, Northwestern University Library. **48** From "Reading Culture from Tobacco Advertisements in Indonesia," by Mimi Nichter et al. Courtesy of Mimi Nichter. **54** TrekPeru. **91** Maria Cheema, Community Renewal Team of Hartford, CT.

10-digit ISBN 1-57766-558-9
13-digit ISBN 978-1-57766-558-8

Printed in the United States of America

7 6 5 4 3 2 1

In loving memory of my parents,
Charlotte and Gerald Biederman

Wine is integral to family meals and celebrations in many cultures, as in this snapshot of a wedding party in Sweden.

Contents

Acknowledgements   ix

**1   An Introduction to the Anthropology of   1
    Addictions and Recovery**
A Note on the Word "Addiction"   5
Ethnography and the Study of Alcohol, Tobacco, and Drugs   5
Physiological Effects of Alcohol, Tobacco, and Drugs   8
Legal Status of Alcohol, Tobacco, and Drugs   10
The Diagnostic Classification Systems
   and Access to Treatment   12
Conclusion   13

2   The Many Faces of Alcohol Use   17
Cross-Cultural Examples of Drinking   18
The Introduction of Alcohol into a Community   21
Alcohol Use and Culture Change   23
Drinking Patterns   25
Costs of Alcohol Abuse   27
Alcohol and Homelessness   28
College Drinking   28
Culture and Drinking   31
Conclusion   32
Experiential Learning Activities   33

3   Tobacco and Its Global Reach   35
Indigenous Uses   35
Diffusion of Tobacco and Smoking   37
Health Consequences   39
Cigarettes as Currency   40
Beliefs about Smoking   41

Camaraderie and Smoking   41
Smoking and Women   42
Smoking and Adolescents   43
Cigarette Marketing Strategies   46
Unintended Consequences of Smoking Bans   49
Conclusion   50
Experiential Learning Activities   50

4   Drug Use and Drug Prohibitions   51
Indigenous Uses of Mind-Altering Drugs:
    The Case of Hallucinogenic Mushrooms, Peyote,
    Coca Leaves, and Ayahuasca   51
Drug Laws as Cultural Artifacts:
    The Case of Morphine, Heroin, Khat, and Marijuana   55
Effect of Law Enforcement and Incarceration   59
Anthropological Research on
    Club Drugs and Prescription Drugs   62
Drug Use Initiation and Continued
    Participation: The Case of Cocaine   67
Ethnography of Suffering:
    The Case of Heroin and Injection Drug Use   69
Ethnographic Research in Response
    to the HIV/AIDS Epidemic   70
Ethnographic Methods to
    Monitor New Drugs: The Case of Illy   72
Conclusion   73
Experiential Learning Activities   73

5   Recovery in Cross-Cultural Perspective   75
The Language of Recovery   76
Current Models of Recovery/Treatment   77
Demonstrating Efficacy in Healing   77
Alcoholics Anonymous:
    A Culturally Malleable Recovery Model   79
When Does a Treatment Not Diffuse?   85
Utilizing Indigenous Culture in Recovery   87
Increasing the Cultural Congruence
    of Treatments and Prevention   90
Changing the Context of Recovery   92
Ethnographic Methods in Drug Treatment
    Outcome Studies   93
Conclusion   94
Experiential Learning Activities   95

6   Concluding Thoughts   97

Bibliography   101
Index   113

Acknowledgements

I am grateful to have had the opportunity to study addiction research through a post-doctoral fellowship of the National Institute of Alcohol Abuse and Alcoholism at the Center for Alcohol and Addiction Research at Brown University.

I am also grateful to the Department of Anthropology/Sociology of Roger Williams University for the opportunity to develop and teach about the anthropology of addictions and recovery within the university core curriculum.

Thank you to Tom Curtin, Senior Editor, and Jeni Ogilvie, Editor, of Waveland Press for their care and expertise in guiding this book. I also thank two anonymous reviewers for their very helpful suggestions.

Thank you to my many colleagues who have helped me think about addictions, recovery, homelessness, and anthropology. Thanks to Bill Zywiak, Eric Hirsch, Tara McLaughlin, Joy Ann Juvelis, Mary Kenny, Liesa Stamm, Anna Chan, Julie Ackerman, Doris Battle, Maria Cheema, Fred Lynn, Nancy Pappas, Lena Rodriguez, and Marybeth MacPhee.

As always, I thank my mentor, Pertti Pelto, whose teaching and wisdom many years ago still inspire me today.

I am lucky to be a part of a loving family and I thank Francine Glasser, Sharon Pacheco, Michael Biederman, Marsha Biederman, my kind husband Morty, and our wonderful sons, daughters-in-law, and grandchildren: Jason, Sophie, Charlotte, and Joseph; Raphael and Cindy; Jonathan, Kathy, Azalea and Selma; and Nathaniel, Linn, and Leon.

Chapter One

An Introduction to the Anthropology of Addictions and Recovery

IG: How much alcohol did you drink last month?
Elderly man: Just a few shots on weekends.
IG: I see.
Elderly man: Now, did you want to know about beer and wine also?

The above exchange took place recently as I was talking with a formerly homeless man in the context of a program evaluation. Although we were speaking the same language, "alcohol" for him meant hard liquor. This example is just a glimpse of the diverse meanings of alcohol, tobacco, and drugs. This book is an introduction to the rich trove of knowledge of these substances throughout time and in various places in the world.

Anthropology, which involves the study of culture, is in many ways well poised to further our understanding of humans and their relationship to alcohol, tobacco, and drugs. As we shall soon see, our beliefs and behaviors toward these mind-altering substances differ greatly from culture to culture as well as within the same culture. Dwight Heath (1996) suggests that the study of alcohol and drugs is a kind of "natural experiment" in that physiological effects of the substances are mediated by the sociocultural systems in which the people live. Good observers, not blinded by cultural biases—the preconceived values of their own culture—are able to describe these behaviors and reactions in the context of the culture(s) in which they occur.

A characteristic of anthropological writing is the fidelity of the descriptions to the events being observed as the anthropologist immerses him- or herself into the community. For example, in 1970 Robert Jarvenpa was in Dawson City, Yukon Territory, Canada, in order to learn the life histories of elderly Han people, who are a First Nation of the Yukon. One night Jarvenpa decided to try making contact with people who had been elusive to him. He entered a bar named The Westminster, in the skid row section of the city.

> After adjusting my eyes to the dim light, I found myself standing in a large empty room. There was an old mahogany bar and a western shuffleboard game, and a half-dozen empty tables, save for one with a patron who had collapsed face down amid a clutter of beer bottles. (Jarvenpa 1998:38)

Making his way further into the bar, Jarvenpa found himself in another room:

> The air was pungent with acrid smoke and stale beer. Squinting through the blue haze, I could not locate Rose and Lucy, but there were many familiar faces. It struck me as poetic justice that the people I had been unsuccessfully pursuing for weeks had been sitting here, a few yards from my lodging, all along. (Jarvenpa 1998:39)

Later in the evening Jarvenpa notes:

> Throughout the evening Harry Reed, a gaunt fellow of mixed Indian-white ancestry, had been wandering into the Westminster and simply collapsing in a drunken stupor upon whatever table, customer, or patch of floor happened to be available. On each occasion he was escorted to the street but somehow always managed to wander back in to create some minor chaos. (Jarvenpa 1998:43)

Notice how Jarvenpa does not use words such as alcoholism, alcohol abuse, alcohol dependence, or any other categories that would obscure his description of a night at The Westminster.

In their ethnographic study of heroin users who are living in filthy encampments in Los Angeles, Philippe Bourgois and Jeff Schonberg (2009) sought to understand the assaults on the body that were the result of injection drug use in the face of repeated infections. Here they observe Hogan, their community consultant,[1] recently released from the hospital after a receiving a life-saving skin graft:

> In the weeks following Hogan's release, it was disconcerting to see him injecting directly into the side of his still-festering skin graft. At first glance, it appeared to be a self-destructing, even masochistic practice, but we soon came to realize that when one's veins are scarred by a lifetime of daily injection and when one's priority is to consume heroin by any means necessary, an abscess is a convenient and effective site for injection. (Bourgois and Schonberg 2009:100)

Through observation and an anthropological lens, Bourgois and Schonberg were able to gain an understanding of Hogan's actions from Hogan's perspective.

The four fields of anthropology—archeology, biological anthropology, linguistic anthropology, and cultural anthropology—have all contributed to our understanding of alcohol, tobacco and drugs. For example, historical archeologist Frederick Smith provides evidence and analyzes the making, drinking, and importance of alcohol in the Caribbean (*Caribbean Rum: A Social and Economic History* 2005). In the field of biological anthropology, Igor and Valerie de Garine explore alcohol use within the wider context of the ingestion of liquids by humans (*Drinking: Anthropological Approaches* 2001). An example of a linguistic analysis is research related to the sale of ecstasy (a club drug that tends to be used by teenagers and young adults at bars, nightclubs, concerts, and parties). Jacinto et al. (2008) found that although the majority of ecstasy users also sold the drug, these young people did not perceive themselves as "dealers" because they were just "hooking up" friends with the drug and did not stray outside of their own social network.

The majority of the examples in this book come from the field of cultural anthropology. Here, anthropologists utilize participant-observation, which is living among the people the researcher is studying. One learns by listening, observing, and participating in daily life as much as possible. Researchers take notes on their observations (usually after the encounter) or use tape recorders to record interviews, with permission, and then analyze their data and write up their observations and conclusions. This end product is an ethnography. Thus, ethnography is the written description of a culture after a period of intensive observation and participant-observation, a hallmark of cultural anthropology, by the fieldworker who has lived within the community. In taking extensive field notes and analyzing them, one is attempting to understand not just the behaviors one can see but also the *worldview* of the culture that makes those behaviors possible. A wonderful description of the more subtle aspects of ethnography is provided by cultural anthropologist Charles Frake, who says that describing a culture

> is not to recount the events of a society but to specify what one must know to make those events maximally probable. The problem is not to state what someone did but to specify the conditions under which it is culturally appropriate to anticipate that he, or persons occupying his role, will render an equivalent performance. (1964:111–112)

In her ethnography of women living in Woodhouse, a Manhattan residence for women who have been homeless, Alisse Waterston comes to know Alma, a woman who is precariously hanging on to this hard-won housing, even though she is "out on the street" much of the time and is often knocking on the other residents' doors in the middle of the night, asking them for money for drugs. One day, Waterston encounters Alma outside:

> Heading toward Woodhouse on Broadway one morning, I catch a glimpse of a familiar figure standing on the street corner, her hand outstretched for a dime or a quarter. It's Alma, a slip of a woman, who looks as if she's had one too many hits of crack this chilly spring morning. Alma's tongue flutters in and out of her dry mouth, as her half-opened eyes do their best to plead for a couple of coins. (Waterston 1999:146)

I was inspired to study alcohol, tobacco, and drug use, misuse, and recovery by my own ongoing anthropological research of homeless populations. It was clear to me, after spending many days and evenings in homeless shelters and soup kitchens, that despite the pervasive substance misuse, there were almost no treatments offered in homeless settings. Further, I found that homelessness is often an *exclusion* criterion in treatment efficacy studies (studies that are designed to measure whether the treatment has had the intended effect) because researchers fear not being able to gain follow-up information from homeless individuals. In fact, many homeless do not stray far from the shelters and soup kitchens that are their lifelines.

As I witnessed addiction treatment research in action, I realized that ethnographic research methods were generally *not* employed in treatment studies, which meant that researchers often missed some crucial cultural understandings. For example, in trying to develop tobacco cessation strategies for homeless people, it is important to recognize the use of cigarettes as barter and currency in the underground economy. Without cigarettes to share, a homeless individual might not, for example, be able to enlist a person to watch his or her things as he or she took a shower in a shelter. However, cigarettes as forms of barter and currency are not often discussed as deterrents to smoking cessation in the treatment literature.

This book was also inspired by teaching the anthropology of addictions and what I saw as a need for a book that provides students with an overarching anthropological perspective. I found that my students were already very aware of the role of alcohol and drugs in their own lives and the lives of family and friends. The students were eager to talk about whom and what they deemed as their cultural role models for excessive drinking leading to drunkenness. After reading some of the literature on drinking cultures throughout the world, they no longer saw their own drinking behaviors as *inevitable* or a function of their age or station in life. Rather, they began to see their drinking as a product of their own culture. This new knowledge was a source of empowerment for them, wherein some considered new drinking patterns for themselves.

A NOTE ON THE WORD "ADDICTION"

For many of us the word *addiction* implies one or more of the following: a compulsion, an obsession, a craving, a psychological dependence, or a physiological dependence so that one believes he or she cannot live without something. As used in everyday language, addiction is applied to a wide variety of substances and conditions, including alcohol, drugs, food, gambling, hoarding, sex, and the Internet. Addiction, especially to alcohol and drugs, is seen as the cause of the downfall of many culture heroes as portrayed in the cinema, in books, and in popular culture. Breaking addiction, with help from others, is an often-told story and one that people refer to as a type of spiritual redemption. An example of a popular portrayal of addiction and recovery is contained in the movie *Walk the Line*, which chronicles the life, music, and struggles with alcohol and drugs of music icon Johnny Cash. With support from those who love him, including mother-in-law Sarah Carter's confrontation with a drug dealer, he finally begins his recovery.

In spite of the pervasive use of the word "addiction," in reference to problems with alcohol, tobacco, and drugs, the medical community most often uses the terms substance *abuse* and substance *dependence*. Abuse and dependence are diagnostic categories that are culturally constructed terms.

More neutral terms for describing the ingesting of alcohol, tobacco, and drugs is substance *use* and *misuse*, which recognizes the great range of humans' relationship to these mind-altering substances. Substances have been and are used throughout the world for healing, for communicating with the spirit world, for rituals and ceremonies, and for enhancing sociability. Substances can also harm individuals or the people around them and can thus also be *misused*. Substance use can lead to what MacAndrew and Edgerton (2003[1969]) call "changes for the worse," which may be illness, squandering family resources, hunger, family and community disintegration, violence, and death.

ETHNOGRAPHY AND THE STUDY OF ALCOHOL, TOBACCO, AND DRUGS

In the early days of anthropology, alcohol, tobacco, and drugs were among the topics discussed in ethnographies. For example, when Ruth Bunzel conducted ethnographic fieldwork among Indian populations in Mexico and Guatemala in the 1930s, she noted how intoxication affected these communities (Bunzel 1940).

Bunzel wrote about the historical role of alcohol and intoxication in pre-conquest Mayan culture that featured drinking as a form of worship to the gods. After the Spanish conquest and the period of intense missionary work of the Catholic Church of the 16th century in indigenous communities (occupied by the people who lived there from the earliest known period) of Mexico and Central America, alcohol continued to be a part of the worship. Bunzel observed:

> In personal rituals libations of *aguardiente* [local alcoholic beverage] are poured out on the altar, and the participants also drink— it would be an offence and insult to the gods not to partake after having invited them. Even in the church, when the priest is looking the other way, *aguardiente* is poured out among the candles and rose petals, and the bottle is passed around. All this is the honoring of an ancient tradition. (1940:362)

Bunzel conducted extensive fieldwork in two Mayan communities where drinking leads to very different outcomes. In one community, that of the Chichicastenago in Guatemala, which Bunzel characterizes as patriarchal (males have the authority) and puritanical (strict social controls sanction the expression sexual desires), she observes competition within the family over land and fear of ancestors. Drinking appears to lead to fights, conflicts, and guilt. The other community, Chamula in Mexico, is much poorer. The land of a family is divided among the children equally. According to Bunzel's observations, there is much drunkenness that leads to stupor and a loss of remembering details of the activities that occur while intoxicated. However, there is generally no aggression or guilt about the drinking. People view being drunk as a good, albeit expensive, activity (Bunzel 1940).

Ethnography has been employed in the study of alcohol, tobacco, and drug use by anthropologists whose work is used in this book to understand substance use in cultures throughout the world. The work of anthropologists may include indigenous substance use, how the substance is a factor in power relationships within a society, the conditions under which people harm themselves and others through substance use, and how people extricate themselves from harmful use. In general, the earliest ethnographies were rendered from long-term living with the people as in the case of Bunzel in two Mayan communities. Later anthropologists used life histories and interviews as well as their observations for their studies in the use of substances. The early anthropological descriptions of alcohol and drinking behavior generally did not include any health outcomes, positive or negative.

Ethnographic research is especially successful in reaching hidden populations, such as those of "street" addicts, in which personal relationships and trust are established and become the catalyst for talking to the researcher and allowing him or her into their world

(Carlson et al. 2009). Ethnographers have witnessed drug use on the street, in "shooting galleries," in homeless encampments, in clubs, and at private parties—a wide social context in which users share cultural understandings. Anthropologists' insights can inform people who design prevention and treatment programs so that the interventions are tailored to the needs of the participants whose drug use is a "lived experience"—that is, participants derive meaning from their drug use. Ethnographic research allows professionals to move from seeing the user as a "marginalized social isolate" to that of being an active player in a living social network. While ethnographers have been successful in viewing the more public "street" addict, they are less successful in researching drug use among middle-class, professional, and suburban residents (Carlson et al. 2009).

In a comprehensive overview of ethnography and drug use, Page and Singer (2010) describe how the ethnography of drug use came of age in the search for effective ways to prevent the transmission of HIV. As ethnographers gained enough trust to witness the actions of intravenous drug users within drug-using settings such as in apartments that were "shooting galleries" for illegal drug use, the researchers could ask, at which point in this process could HIV transmission be reduced? For example, could clean needles be distributed to the people in charge of the shooting galleries, and would they promote the use of clean and uncontaminated needles?

While ethnography has been utilized in studies of drug use, tobacco use, alcohol use, and treatment, its potential for understanding what happens once a person *leaves* a treatment program has not been fully realized. More research needs to follow the person out the door of the treatment center and back into the community, as the individual faces the same conditions that preceded his or her treatment, often triggering a relapse.

Living and learning in the community of study often leads to an appreciation of the categories of phenomena within the community's culture, which may be little known to outsiders, and thus are called *emic*[2] categories. In the field of addictions research, a good example of an emic/insider category would be "flop" (a place to stay for the night). Whereas an outsider may understand the term to mean a cheap hotel, a mission, a shelter, or an empty railroad car, the insider perspective is different. The chronically intoxicated men of James Spradley's classic study *You Owe Yourself a Drunk* (1970) understood the various dimensions of "flops." In this ethnography, Spradley follows the men as they drift through detoxification centers, jails, and the cheap housing of Seattle's skid row. Spradley finds that the decision of where to stay for the night depends on many factors including how one's body would be positioned for sleep (lying down, sitting up, supposed to sit up but may lie down); intoxication allowed or not (must be sober, must be drunk, any state of intoxication allowed); and whether listening to sermons or praying is important or necessary as a condition to spending the night (Spradley 1970). In the world of the "urban nomads," to use Spradley's term, a "flop" means more than just a general place to spend the night; knowing the insider perspective gives the outsider a better understanding of the many things to consider in choosing where to lay one's head for the night.

Before proceeding further, we will briefly review the physiological effects of alcohol, tobacco, and drugs; the graduations of legality of these substances in the United States and in other parts of the world; and the widely used diagnostic categories of substance use disorders. A discussion of these three broad topics, which may be thought of as a very brief "Addictions 101" course serves as a backdrop for our study of addictions and treatment.

PHYSIOLOGICAL EFFECTS OF ALCOHOL, TOBACCO, AND DRUGS

In addition to understanding how substances have been used and at times misused in various cultures we need to know some of the physiological effects of alcohol, tobacco, and drugs on humans. The effects are dependent on the quantity and frequency of use, on variation in user reaction to the drugs, as well as on whether the substance is legal or illegal; the latter designation can in fact make use much more dangerous. For example, heroin, which is illegal, is sold in the underground economy without any regulation or quality assurance. People who buy heroin do not know the actual strength of the drug or its true contents (it has been known to be diluted with strychnine and other poisons), so they are at risk of overdose or death (NIDA 2010a). The criminalization of drugs—making it a crime to buy sell, possess, or use certain drugs—has resulted in a lucrative black market drug trade that often leaves violence and death in its wake.

We will use research pharmacologist Carlton Erickson's definition of drugs as "a chemical other than food or water that produces a therapeutic or nontherapeutic pharmacological action (effect) in the body" (2007:93). Drugs can be medicinal (such as aspirin), legal (such as nicotine), or illegal (such as heroin). A drug can fall into more than one category, as is the case with cocaine, which is therapeutic (legal) when used as an anesthetic for eye surgery, but is nontherapeutic (illegal) when used to get high. The work of Erickson is particularly useful as he has separated the politically charged law enforcement concerns from the physiological effects of the drugs.

Alcohol, tobacco, and drugs create changes in the central nervous system (CNS), which consists of the brain and spinal cord and which coordinates the activity of the entire nervous system. *Stimulants* are drugs that increase CNS activity and cause people to experience states such as euphoria, increased motor activity, talkativeness, inability to sleep, and repetitive behavior (Erickson 2007). An example of a stimulant is cocaine, which can be administered intravenously or through snorting or smoking. It has a high potential for abuse and dependence. It is important to note that any drug taken by injection increases the risk of infection through needle contamination with HIV, hepatitis, and other organisms.

Depressants are drugs that slow nerve cell activity in the CNS (Erickson 2007). This slowing down, however, may cause a speeding up or a lack of inhibition in other areas. An example of this is the social euphoria caused by the first one or two drinks of alcohol, followed by drowsiness, slowing of reaction time, and depression with later drinks. Another example of a depressant is the opiate class of drugs that includes morphine and heroin. Opiates are used legally to treat pain, coughs, and diarrhea. Chronic use of opiates does not produce the organ damage of alcohol or tobacco; however, there is a high potential for dependence, and there is the danger of accidental overdose. The opiates are characterized by rapid tolerance (needing to use larger amounts to produce the same effect) and severe withdrawal after chronic use (Erickson 2007).

Alcohol is believed to be socially and medically beneficial when used in moderation (see "Alcohol: Balancing Risks and Benefits" [2009] for a discussion on the health implications of moderate alcohol use). In large doses, over time, alcohol causes damage to the liver, heart, brain, esophagus, and stomach. Death can occur from an overdose, from suffocating on one's vomit or from the effect of alcohol on the areas of the brain that control breathing. Death can also occur from withdrawal-associated seizures once a long-term heavy drinker stops drinking. It is important, therefore, for long-term, heavy drinkers to detoxify from alcohol under medical supervision in order to avoid seizures associated with withdrawal (Erickson 2007).

The relationship between drinking and driving is well known. Hingson and Winter (2003) report that in the United States 41% of people fatally injured in traffic crashes were in alcohol-related crashes in which the driver or pedestrian had consumed alcohol. In Canada and the United States, the legal Blood Alcohol Concentration (BAC) limit is .08, which means that it is an offense to drive at a BAC of .08 or higher, whether or not the driver or operator exhibits visible signs of intoxication. Other countries have lower legal limits, such as .02% for Sweden, and .05% for France. There are countries, too, that recognize that any alcohol consumed can impair driving, and so there is zero tolerance for a BAC of anything over 0. Such countries with zero tolerance include

Armenia, Brazil, Nigeria, Iran, and Japan (Worldwide BAC Limits). On average, a male of 180 pounds drinking four drinks (defined as, for example, a 12-ounce beer or one glass, 4 ounces of wine) in a row would result in a BAC of .08, and a woman of 120 pounds drinking two drinks in a row would result in a BAC of .08 (http://www.ou.edu/oupd/bac.htm).

Nicotine is a highly toxic drug that is packaged in drug-delivery systems of cigars and cigarettes (Erickson 2007). Nicotine increases one's heart rate, blood pressure, energy, and mental alertness. It also causes rapid or irregular heartbeats, adverse pregnancy outcomes, chronic lung disease, cardiovascular disease, stroke, and cancer (NIDA 2010b). Nicotine is the chemical in cigarettes that causes the dependence; the tar in the cigarettes increases the smoker's risk of lung cancer, emphysema, and bronchial disorders (NIDA n.d.).

A useful research question is: which drugs have the greatest probability of dependency (sometimes termed *dependence liability*)? The answer varies among researchers. In one liability listing, the estimated proportion of users who will become dependent is: nicotine 32%; heroin 23%; cocaine 17%; alcohol 15%; stimulants 11%; cannabis 9%; psychedelics 5%; and inhalants 4% (Anthony, Warner and Kessler 1994). Other dependence liability ratings rank (in order) heroin, nicotine, cocaine, and alcohol as the highest in terms of potential for dependence (Erickson 2007). Another ranking lists cocaine and amphetamines as the highest liability of becoming dependent, nicotine and opiates next, with alcohol, benzodiazepines, and barbiturates next (Erickson 2007).

LEGAL STATUS OF ALCOHOL, TOBACCO, AND DRUGS

The U.S. Congress enacted the Controlled Substance Act (CSA) in the early 1970s as part of the Comprehensive Drug Abuse Prevention and Control Act. The CSA provides the government with a means to control the manufacture and distribution of substances (drugs) it considers abusive or harmful. The controlled substances are categorized according to five tiers, called schedules, based on the government's perception of each substance's medical value, harmfulness, and potential for abuse and addiction. In reality, drug schedules are themselves artifacts of culture; that is, they reflect current notions about each substance and the vagaries of attitudes toward drugs. The schedule numbers, I through IV, refer to the categories designated by the US Drug Enforcement Administration (DEA), which was created by President Richard Nixon in 1973 in order to establish a single, unified command for "an all-out global war on the drug menace" (http://www.justice.gov/dea/history.htm). Neither alcohol nor tobacco is a scheduled drug.[3]

As mentioned above, the defining characteristics of a drug's status is its potential for dependence and abuse as well as whether or not there are known medical benefits from the drug. There are exceptions, as in the ritual and religious use of peyote by members of the Native American Church (Jones 2007), which has received an exemption from its Schedule I status.

Schedule I and II drugs have a high potential for abuse. Schedule I drugs are available for research only and have no approved medical use. Schedule II drugs are available only by prescription, can be used therapeutically, and have a high potential for abuse. Schedule III drugs have some potential for abuse. Schedule IV drugs have low potential for abuse. Schedule V drugs have the lowest potential for abuse, and some may be sold over the counter (NIDA 2010b; Erickson 2007).

Some of the health risks are directly related to the route of drug administration. For example, injection drug use can increase the risk of infection through needle contamination with staphylococci, HIV, hepatitis, and other organisms (NIDA 2010b).

The Designation of Drug Schedule I–V in the United States		
Schedule Number	Description	Examples
I	Has no approved medical use; has high potential for abuse, available for research only (note: although there are 14 states in which it is legal to use marijuana for medical purposes, it remains a Schedule 1 drug).	heroin, LSD, marijuana
II	High potential for abuse, available by prescription only	cocaine, morphine, amphetamines
III	Has a medical use and a low to moderate risk of physical dependence but a high risk for psychological dependence	anabolic steroids, ketamine, marinol
IV	Has medical use and a low potential for abuse	Xanax, Librium, Valium
V	Has medical use and a lower potential for abuse; some are over-the-counter drugs	cough suppressants with codeine, and preparations to treat diarrhea that may contain opium
Adapted from Mignon, Faiia, Myers, and Rubington (2009:15).		

THE DIAGNOSTIC CLASSIFICATION SYSTEMS
AND ACCESS TO TREATMENT

People trying to extricate themselves from substance use may need to be diagnosed as having a substance use disorder prior to receiving treatment. Diagnosis frequently entails the use of medically sanctioned classification systems. As in the case of legal classifications, diagnostic classification systems are a part of the broad social context of substance use and misuse.

The two most widely used systems of classification of substance use disorders from repetitive substance use are the World Health Organization (WHO) International Classification of Diseases (now in its tenth edition [ICD-10]) used throughout the world and the American Psychiatric Association's Diagnostic and Statistical Manual of Mental Disorders (now in its fourth edition [DSM-IV]) used in North America (Saunders 2006). These codifications have power in that the diagnosis becomes the gatekeeper for those who may receive treatment and who can have the treatment paid for by medical insurance. Diagnostic categories also standardize the terms used for research in, for example, efficacy studies of various treatments for substance abuse and dependence.

When we compare the six ICD-10 criteria for the diagnosis of substance dependence (p. 14) with the seven DSM-IV criteria for the diagnosis of substance dependence (p. 15) we see that there is much congruence between them. Both include criteria for increased tolerance for the substance, meaning that an individual needs increased amounts of the substance to achieve the desired effect and experiences a diminished effect with continued use. Both sets of criteria also include reference to physiological withdrawal symptoms when substance use is stopped or reduced. The ICD-10 includes reference to a sense of compulsion not mentioned in the DSM-IV.

When we compare the criteria for the diagnosis of harmful use listed in the ICD-10 (p. 15) and the criteria for the diagnosis of substance abuse of DSM-IV (p. 16) we see more differences between the two classification systems. The harmful use criteria of ICD-10 emphasizes the adverse health and mental health consequences of use. Although the adverse social consequences are acknowledged (such as losing one's job), the social consequences themselves are not sufficient to justify a diagnosis of harmful use. The substance abuse criteria of DSM-IV are more explicit in the kinds of social and interpersonal problems that the substance use may be causing the individual, including legal problems, to justify the abuse diagnosis. Both the harmful use of ICD-10 as well as substance abuse of DSM-IV are considered to be less reliable as concepts than dependence, meaning that there is lower agreement between independent raters when diagnosing the same person (Saunders 2006).

CONCLUSION

It is difficult to discuss or even categorize substances and substance use without applying our own cultural prism to their realms. Anthropology helps us view substance use in various parts of the world and at various points in human history without being blinded by our cultural biases. However, there are at least two traps into which we may fall in viewing substances from an anthropological point of view. The first is *romanticizing* substance use, especially in indigenous cultures and cultures as they existed in the past and are described orally or in diaries and field notes of observers. These reports tend not to include adverse reactions, not due to any calculated omission but because the substance use was often observed in communities that lacked access to health care and in communities with low life expectancies. Therefore, people in these communities did not necessarily realize that substance use could be the cause of physical and mental ailments as well as death.

The second trap is *demonizing* substance use. A typical library or Internet search on topics of alcohol, tobacco, and drugs will quickly unearth information about dangerous, illegal, and other negative aspects of these substances—abuse, dependence, and criminality—all of which are reinforced by mass media. In the United States, the leading agencies within the National Institutes of Health (NIH), whose mission is to "seek fundamental knowledge about the nature and behavior of living systems and the application of that knowledge to enhance health, lengthen life, and reduce the burdens of illness and disability" (http://www.nih.gov/about/mission.htm), have names—the National Institute on Alcohol Abuse and Alcoholism (NIAAA) and the National Institute on Drug Abuse (NIDA)—which signal chief concerns, rather than possible positive outcomes.

This book is concerned with how culture affects our relationships with mind-altering substances and recognizes that there is a wide range of individual behaviors in relation to alcohol, tobacco, and drugs *within* each culture. Concepts are drawn from an extensive body of literature that deals with explanations for and variations of use, misuse, and recovery among individuals.

In the pages that follow we will look at a *sampling* of the literature on alcohol, tobacco, and drug use among the great trove of anthropological work on substances. Much though not all of the research presented here was undertaken by anthropologists in the course of their fieldwork. The chapter on recovery reflects my ongoing interests in culture's role, as people try to extricate themselves from use that is detrimental to them or to their communities. At the end of each chapter are suggested experiential activities that enable learning about substance use, misuse, and recovery cross-culturally. These activities are ones that I have utilized in my classes over many years of teaching anthropology. Students tell me that when they experience learning in this kind of hands-on, visceral manner, they gain insights that no amount of reading can convey.

Criteria for the ICD-10 Diagnosis of Substance Dependence

A definite diagnosis of dependence should usually be made only if three or more of the following have been present together at some time during the previous year:

(a) a strong desire or sense of compulsion to take the substance;

(b) difficulties in controlling substance-taking behaviour in terms of its onset, termination, or levels of use;

(c) a physiological withdrawal state when substance use has ceased or been reduced, as evidenced by: the characteristic withdrawal syndrome for the substance; or use of the same (or a closely related) substance with the intention of relieving or avoiding withdrawal symptoms;

(d) evidence of tolerance, such that increased doses of the psychoactive substances are required in order to achieve effects originally produced by lower doses (clear examples of this are found in alcohol- and opiate-dependent individuals who may take daily doses sufficient to incapacitate or kill nontolerant users);

(e) progressive neglect of alternative pleasures or interests because of psychoactive substance use, increased amount of time necessary to obtain or take the substance or to recover from its effects;

(f) persisting with substance use despite clear evidence of overtly harmful consequences, such as harm to the liver through excessive drinking, depressive mood states consequent to periods of heavy substance use, or drug-related impairment of cognitive functioning; efforts should be made to determine that the user was actually, or could be expected to be, aware of the nature and extent of the harm.

(http://www.who.int/substance_abuse/terminology/ICD10ClinicalDiagnosis.pdf)

Criteria for the DSM-IV Diagnosis of Substance Dependence

A maladaptive pattern of substance use leading to clinically significant impairment or distress, as manifested by three (or more) of the following, occurring any time in the same 12-month period:

1. Tolerance, as defined by either of the following:
    (a) A need for markedly increased amounts of the substance to achieve intoxication or the desired effect.
    (b) Markedly diminished effect with continued use of the same amount of the substance.
2. Withdrawal, as manifested by either of the following:
    (a) The characteristic withdrawal syndrome for the substance.
    (b) The same (or closely related) substance is taken to relieve or avoid withdrawal symptoms.
3. The substance is often taken in larger amounts or over a longer period than intended.
4. There is a persistent desire or unsuccessful efforts to cut down or control substance use.
5. A great deal of time is spent in activities necessary to obtain the substance (e.g., visiting multiple doctors or driving long distances), use the substance (e.g., chain-smoking), or recover from its effects.
6. Important social, occupational, or recreational activities are given up or reduced because of substance use.
7. The substance use is continued despite knowledge of having a persistent physical or psychological problem that is likely to have been caused or exacerbated by the substance (e.g., current cocaine use despite recognition of cocaine-induced depression, or continued drinking despite recognition that an ulcer was made worse by alcohol consumption).

DSM-IV criteria for substance dependence could be with physiologic dependence (evidence of tolerance or withdrawal) or without physiologic dependence (no evidence of tolerance or withdrawal).

(*Diagnostic and Statistical Manual of Mental Disorders, Fourth Edition, Text Revision.* 2000:197)

Criteria for the ICD-10 Diagnosis of Harmful Use

A pattern of psychoactive substance use that is causing damage to health. The damage may be physical (e.g., hepatitis following injection of drugs) or mental (e.g., depressive episodes secondary to heavy alcohol intake). Harmful use commonly, but not invariably, has adverse social consequences; social consequences in themselves, however, are not sufficient to justify a diagnosis of harmful use. The term was introduced in ICD-10 and supplanted "non-dependent use" as a diagnostic term. The closest equivalent in other diagnostic systems (e.g., DSM-IV) is substance abuse, which usually includes social consequences.

(http://www.who.int/substance_abuse/terminology/definition2/en/index.html)

Criteria for the DSM-IV Diagnosis of Substance Abuse

A. A maladaptive pattern substance use leading to clinically significant impairment or distress, as manifested by one (or more) of the following, occurring within a 12-month period:

(1) recurrent substance use resulting in a failure to fulfill major role obligations at work, school, or home (e.g., repeated absences or poor work performance related to substance use; substance-related absences, suspensions, or expulsions from school; neglect of children or household)

(2) recurrent substance use in situations in which it is physically hazardous (e.g., driving an automobile or operating a machine when impaired by substance use)

(3) recurrent substance-related legal problems (e.g., arrests for substance-related disorderly conduct)

(4) continued substance use despite having persistent or recurrent social or interpersonal problems caused or exacerbated by the effects of the substance (e.g., arguments with spouse about consequences of Intoxication, physical fights)

B. The symptoms have never met the criteria for Substance Dependence for this class of substance.

(*Diagnostic and Statistical Manual of Mental Disorders, Fourth Edition, Text Revision*. 2000:199)

Notes

[1] We use the word *community consultant* to refer to those individuals who spend time with anthropologists as they learn the culture which is the focus of the study. Earlier works used the term "key informant" for this same role.

[2] The term *emic* is derived from the word *phonemic*. A *phoneme* is a short sound that is best heard by a native speaker, for example, a vowel sound in French may be difficult for a non-native speaker of French to hear. Thus, an emic category is one that is well understood by natives of the culture and is an understanding that anthropologists try to master once immersed in long term research.

[3] A full discussion of the harmful effects of alcohol, tobacco, and drugs (both licit and illicit) can be found on the websites of the National Institute on Alcohol Abuse and Alcoholism (for alcohol), abbreviated as NIAAA (http://www.niaaa.nih.gov) and of the National Institute on Drug Abuse (for drugs and tobacco), abbreviated as NIDA (http://www.nida.nih.gov). Both are a part of the National Institutes of Health, referred to as NIH (http://www.nih.gov), which describes itself as the steward of medical and behavioral research for the United States.

Chapter Two

The Many Faces
of Alcohol Use

The rich ethnographic record of alcohol use in many societies throughout the world constitutes the origin of the field of the anthropology of addiction. The ethnographic observations of alcohol consumption (drinking) range from its role in community-building to its role in unleashing expressions of aggression and violence. A fascinating area of cross-cultural study is how alcohol was introduced to people who did not drink it until it was brought to them by outsiders. The consequences of the introduction of alcohol appear to be dependent on why and by whom it was introduced.

Craig MacAndrew and Robert Edgerton's landmark cross-cultural study of drinking behavior in the 1960s resulted in *Drunken Comportment* (2003[1969]). They successfully challenged the commonly held belief at the time that the intake of alcohol *necessarily*, because of its physiological effects, caused changes for the worse. Rather, through an examination of history and culture, they found that drunken comportment, or how people act when they drink to intoxication, appears to be dependent on how they *learned* to drink, from whom, and if they use drinking as a culturally sanctioned "time out." MacAndrew and Edgerton document that drinking, including becoming "falling down drunk," is socially integrative in some cultures but induces "changes for the worse" in others.

In this chapter we will look at the diffusion of alcohol and its variable effects on groups of people. Examples from Latin America, Native North America, South Africa, Eastern Europe, and among homeless communities introduce us to a variety of drinking cultures. We will end the chapter with a look at drinking behavior of a familiar cultural group: college students.

17

CROSS-CULTURAL EXAMPLES OF DRINKING

The Camba of Eastern Bolivia

The ethnographic record presents numerous examples of drinking that result in states of inebriation without aggression and expressions of hostility. For example, the Camba are a group of indigenous people who live in eastern Bolivia and whose drinking has been studied by Dwight Heath. When Heath (1958) first met the Camba, their drinking occurred at drinking parties over the weekend or on holidays. These drinking parties appeared to be the Camba's primary social network outside of the mother–children relationship. The alcohol they drank had a high concentration of pure alcohol, or ethanol (about 89%); people's sweat smelled of alcohol; and people regularly passed out. They did not, however, exhibit the aggression, boisterousness, clowning, or sentimentality often seen in other cultures with heavy drinking. As Heath observed:

> Drinking itself was so formalized as to be a secular ritual. With only one bottle and a single glass in use at any time, person A (the host, who had bought the first couple of bottles) would pour a tumbler (about 300 g.) of alcohol (the 178-proof raw fuel produced by local sugar refineries). . . . He would then stand in front of person B. . . . After nodding slightly, A would say in the local dialect, "Health" or "To your health," drink half of the glass in one quick draft, and hand it to B. B returned the toast and emptied the glass in a single gulp, after which A would sit down. B would refill the glass and toast C. And so it went, hour after hour, day and night, until either supply ran out or people would be called to work. . . . When a participant passed out, he or she was simply left while the party continued; on waking up or coming to, that person rejoined without comment. (Heath 2000:162)

Heath's observations about Camba drinking were embedded within his study of land reform and social change (Gladwell 2010:70). He was not specifically studying Camba drinking and thus had no preconceived categories in which to fit Camba drinking.

Pulque in Tescopa, Mexico

Pulque is a fermented drink that contains about 6% alcohol and has been present in Mexico from preconquest times. William and Claudia Madsen (1979) observed the production and drinking of pulque within the town of Tescopa, a Nahuat village that is about one hour's drive from Mexico City. When the Madsens conducted their research, people spoke Nahuatl in their homes, though most were bilingual in Spanish. The following describes how pulque was produced:

The fields which produce maize, beans, and squash are outlined by rows of maguey plants. When a maguey reaches maturity and begins to send up its thick flower stock, this growth is cut off at its base, leaving a cavity which daily fills with fluid intended for the stock. The fluid, called *aguamiel* is milked daily by sucking it into a large, perforated gourd and letting it flow into a container. Then the *aguamiel* is added to the *pulque* barrel in the home, where fermentation takes place. The fermented *pulque* at the bottom of the barrel and the human saliva mixed with the *aguamiel* initiate the process of fermentation which produces *pulque*. (Madsen and Madsen 1979:42)

Pulque was consumed at every meal, and pregnant women took an extra serving for their unborn child. Drinking and drunkenness occurred during family and community fiestas, including saints' days, weddings, house warmings, wakes, baptisms, and confirmations. Hangovers the next day were dealt with by rest, herbal teas, and more pulque. The agricultural work of the community could wait until the person recovered. The Madsens found that a drunken man might beat his wife, which at the time of their fieldwork was sanctioned by the community.

Alcohol Use in Ixtepeji, Mexico

In a study of the worldview of the people of the Zapotec town of Ixtepeji in the state of Oaxaca, Mexico, in the late-1960s and early-1970s, Michael Kearney found a profoundly ambivalent attitude toward drinking. Alcohol was utilized in celebrations during the many fiestas that marked the yearly calendar of Ixtepeji. As he came to know the community, people told Kearney their emic categorizations of intoxication, ranging from becoming sociable to falling down:

The first stage is called *sangre de mono* or *sangre de chango* (monkey blood). A person in a state of sangre de chango is described as opening up; he "opens his confidence," becomes sentimental, and says things he does not ordinarily say. He is also apt to become uninhibited, friendly, and cavort about—thus the term "monkey blood." But as he continues, he passes into a stage of *sangre de león* (lion blood), which is induced by *tragos de valor*, or literally "swallows of valor." In this phase the drinker becomes belligerent, argumentative, and perhaps wants to fight; he drinks faster and soon enters the next stage of *sangre de cuche* (pig blood). He now loses control of his faculties, staggers, perhaps vomits, and eventually falls into a stupor, most likely to be left to lie where he has fallen. (Kearney 1986:96)

When Kearney asked his community consultants why they drink, they gave him several reasons, including: there is no other diversion in town, one talks better while intoxicated, alcohol produces happiness and excitement, and alcohol removes sadness.

Women Drinkers in a Mayan Community

Otelia, a Mayan woman, sang the following song to anthropologist Christine Eber during Eber's fieldwork in the Mayan highland town of San Pedro Chenalhó in the state of Chiapas, Mexico, during the 1980s and 1990s.

I am a drunk woman
I am a drunk girl
Yes, yes.
Yes, I am a woman
I don't have father
I am a drunk woman
I am a drunk girl
That's the way it is,
That's the way it is
I am going, girl,
I am going, mother,
I'm really going, yes.
I'm on my way to worthlessness,
I'm on my way to death,
I'm a woman, yes,
I'm leaving, yes. (Eber 2000:135)

This mournful song was often sung by older women when they were drunk, accompanied by abruptly raising their hand at the conclusion of the song in order to vent their anger. Eber's study focused on the role of alcohol among indigenous women in a Mayan community. Her work fills an important gap in our understanding of the full impact of alcohol from a woman's perspective.

Eber found many households in San Pedro Chenalhó affected by the chronic drinking of husband, wife, or both. Inevitably it meant that children suffered as well. Women had long been associated with producing and selling the native ceremonial drink *chicha*, which was originally made from fermented maize and is now made from fermented sugar. Although one can get drunk on chicha, it generally has a low alcohol content and is relatively inexpensive. After the Spanish conquest, the colonialists introduced rum to the indigenous population along with nonceremonial drinking to intoxication. By the time Eber observed women like Otelia who were chronic drinkers, women were drinking and selling both chicha and rum. Eber also documented a social movement in which people substituted soda for rum in their rituals. This substitution appeared to preserve a cultural practice of celebration while avoiding the deleterious effects of alcohol for those who participated in the ceremonies with soda.

Drinking and Pregnancy in South Africa

Heavy drinking in Western Cape Province, South Africa, may be related to the legacy of the *dop*. The dop is the several-centuries-old system of partially paying farmworkers in the region with alcohol on a daily basis. The word "dop" comes from the Afrikaans word for drink (May, Gossage, and Brooke et al. 2005). Although this system was formally outlawed many years ago, drinking heavily on the weekends in groups is still widespread. Although the people are poor, there is enough money to buy beer and wine.

The highest rates of fetal alcohol syndrome (FAS) have been reported in South Africa, where FAS has been reported to be 46 cases per 1,000 births in Western Cape Province (May, et al. 2005). Fetal alcohol spectrum disorder (FASD) includes fetal alcohol syndrome (FAS) and the less severe fetal alcohol effects (FAE). These fetal alcohol disorders result from a mother's drinking during her pregnancy. The results of FAS can be facial defects; missing fingers, toes, or kidneys; a low IQ; a small brain; and a shortened lifespan (Erickson 2007:129). The US Department of Health and Human Services recommends not drinking at all if a woman is pregnant or is planning on becoming pregnant.

In South Africa mothers of the FAS babies were more likely to come from alcohol-abusing families, to drink heavily on the weekends, and to smoke during their pregnancy. These mothers tended to be small in size, and they were poorer, less religious, and had less education than the mothers whose babies did not have FAS (May et al. 2005). May and his colleagues recommend implementing an intense public health education campaign that would educate the population about FAS as a preventable condition. Including knowledge about the dop legacy, as a reminder of European domination of South Africa, could be helpful in enabling the population to understand that drinking so heavily was not a part of their culture before European contact.

THE INTRODUCTION OF ALCOHOL INTO A COMMUNITY

How drinking was introduced to communities is important in the development of drinking cultures (as noted above for South Africa) and is well illustrated by the following historical examples for the Lakota Sioux of North America and the Trukese of Micronesia.

Beatrice Medicine (2007) describes the disastrous introduction of alcohol to the Lakota Sioux and other hunting and gathering North American indigenous groups. Apart from some of the southwestern

Indian nations, Amerindians did not make their own alcohol before European contact, which occurred between 1790 and 1830. Alcohol was introduced by both the French and American fur traders and used as an enticement in their competition for the fur produced by the animals hunted by the Lakota Sioux. In a history of the Brulé Sioux (one of the tribes of the Lakota Nation) and their relationship with competing American and French fur trade companies, Hyde (1961) notes:

> As was always the case when competition for Indian trade was keen, the rival companies made free use of liquor. They drenched the Sioux camps with alcohol; they sold it at a loss and even gave it away in kegs to the Sioux to win them away from rival traders. (33)

As alcohol was now used as currency for the fur and the Lakota Sioux drank to intoxication, tribal chiefs, such as Spotted Tail, refused to bring their band to a camp for food rations because of the accessibility of alcohol. Alcohol became an effective tool in the suppression of native peoples by rendering them less effective in fighting the encroachment of Europeans (Medicine 2007).

Today Native Americans have the highest rates of alcohol-related deaths of all US ethnic groups (Ehlers 2007). According to the Indian Health Service, the age-adjusted death rate in 1992 was 5.6 times higher among American Indians than in the general US population; chronic liver disease was 3.9 times higher; and alcohol-related fatalities were 3 times higher (Beauvais 1998: 255). Among the historical explanations for the high toll that drinking has taken on American Indians are: emulating the heavy drinking of the European colonists who introduced alcohol; the loss of culture, land, and economic independence due to the Euro-American westward expansion; and the devastating effects (on entire families), of Indian children being forced to attend boarding school and their experiences there (see Beauvais 1998 for an excellent review).

Mac Marshall's pioneering work among the Trukese people of the Carolina Islands in Micronesia underlines the various meanings of drunken comportment. Before extensive contact with the Europeans, the Trukese had no experience with alcohol, as this Protestant missionary, Reverend Robert Logan, observed in 1886:

> The people are utterly without intoxicants of any kind. Toddy, from cocoa-sap, is very easily made: but the people throw it away when it ferments, think it spoiled. This seems strange, as they will eat fish after they smell so badly as nearly to knock one over. (Marshall 1979b:37)

The Europeans who came to the islands in the 19th century introduced alcohol to the Trukese, who were known as warriors, having attacked nearly every whaling ship from the mid-16th to the mid-19th centuries (Marshall 1979b:38). The whalers who did come ashore during the mid-1800s appeared to use their shore leave on the islands as a release after being cooped up on a ship for so long and drank heavily and became boisterous and aggressive. This may have had a powerful role model effect when the Trukese began to drink. In the seven months of ethnographic study in 1976, Marshall found that young men used the weekends for heavy drinking and fighting. They appeared to see their drinking as a "time out" and as an excuse to curse out the elders and show their manhood. At the time of his study, Marshall reports that among the 15- to 24-year-old males, only one-third were in school and there was a 75% unemployment rate. Marshall calls these young intoxicated men "weekend warriors," and he hypothesizes that they were expressing their legendary fighting abilities within the confines of a drinking spree. Marshall observes:

> Trukese recognize that most young men who drink and subsequently engage in weekend warfare do so to impress others—particularly young ladies. . . . Everyone knows in Truk that drunks are dangerous, crazy, just like animals, and beyond reason because they cannot "hear" anything that is said to them. (Marshall 1979b:113)

ALCOHOL USE AND CULTURE CHANGE

How alcohol is used over time within a culture is in many ways a barometer of culture change. Three examples of change in alcohol use from the ethnographic record are the Tohono O'odham people (formerly the Papago) of the southwestern United States who went from drinking wine made of the saguaro cactus to drinking distilled liquor in the 1930s (Underhill 1985), the Irish Tinkers as they became a more settled people living on the outskirts of Irish cities (Gmelch 1985), and the Nganasan and Dolgan people of Russian Siberia, who went from a pastoral, hunting, fishing, and trapping communities to a settled communities with widespread unemployment (Ziker 2002).

In 1938 anthropologist Ruth Underhill observed the wine ceremony of the Tohono O'odham people:

> When the wine was ready for consumption, the Indians gathered around in a large circle outside the sacred rain house. From the rain house four cupbearers emerged, each carrying a basket containing the wine. These baskets they brought to four medicine men, each of whom was sitting in the circle at one of the four points of the compass. The medicine men then proceeded ritually to cleanse the wine by rubbing their hands around the baskets. Next, a speech of admonition was delivered to all the participants, stressing the Papago virtues of peacefulness and harmony. Following this, the baskets were passed counterclockwise around the circle, a

cupbearer dipping out a portion for each participant and saying as
he offered the beverage, "Drink friend. Grow beautifully drunk."
(cited in MacAndrew and Edgerton 2003:38–39)

Thus, although the men did become "falling down drunk," from
the historical accounts it appears that people were good tempered
while drunk (MacAndrew and Edgerton, 2003[1969]). The words for
drunk and dizzy in the O'odham language are considered to be sacred
words. However, by the 1930s, the Tohono O'odham also had access to
hard liquor and, without the ceremonial context of drinking, being
drunk became disruptive and dangerous. Thus, for a while, there were
two, side-by-side kinds of drinking to intoxication, one apparently
innocuous and the other not.

By the 1940s, children of the Tohono O'odham learned to fear the
wine ceremonies, as noted by ethnographers Joseph, Spicer, and
Chesky (1949):

> During the fiesta the small child learns of a new danger. He finds
> that men, perhaps his father and uncles, at times, behave strangely.
> His female relatives snatch him out of the way and whisper, "Drunk!"
> in the same tone they use to warn him of ghosts. He learns to run
> away when drunks lurch near him and to ignore them completely
> when they accost him; sometimes he witnesses brawls or other vio-
> lence. (cited in MacAndrew and Edgerton 2003[1969]:41–42)

In 1971–1972, anthropologists George and Sharon Gmelch lived
in an Irish Travellers' (or Tinkers, as they are also known) encampment and observed alcohol's toll on families as they heard men beating
their wives during the night and saw men spending much of the household income at the pub (Gmelch 1985). Piecing together oral histories
and historical documents, Gmelch demonstrates how the Travellers
went from being itinerant workers going from farm to farm fixing the
milk cans and other household items (thus the name "Tinkers") to
urban dwellers due in part to the introduction of plastics, which made
the tinker trade obsolete. Now the Travellers moved with their horse-
drawn caravans to the more urban areas, hoping to participate in selling used items. No longer adequately employed, the men depended
more and more on their wives who obtained income through welfare
and begging. According to Gmelch, this role reversal and the lack of
anything else to do increased the drinking and drunkenness of the
Travellers so that alcohol was now consuming a significant part of a
family's resources, and domestic violence followed nights of drinking.

Another instance of increased alcohol use is documented by John
Ziker (2002) who lived with the Dolgan and Nganasan people in the
Siberian Arctic in the 1990s as they adjusted to the post-Soviet government. Even before the current era, Ziker documents the increase in
violent deaths including accidents, poisonings, trauma, homicide, and

suicide associated with alcohol beginning in the 1930s as the Dolgan and Nganasan people were being forced from hunting and gathering into employment by the state in settled communities (Ziker 2002:86). After the collapse of the USSR in 1991, mortality increased among the Dolgan and Nganasan people as unemployment increased and the support of state enterprises was lost. Violent deaths were most numerous during periods of inactivity and when alcohol was most available (Ziker 2002:97).

DRINKING PATTERNS

Drinking Careers

The term "drinking careers" was introduced by Kunitz and Levy (1994) in reference to the life course of people who are heavy drinkers. The use of the word *career* as they use it does not suggest choice, but it does suggest patterns. Kunitz and Levy had the opportunity to interview and re-interview 112 Navajo men and women with a 25-year span between the two interviews. The men and women came from three different groups: people living most traditionally within the plateau area of the Navajo reservation; people who were wage workers in Tuba City, an agency town on the Navajo reservation; and people from an alcohol treatment program of the Public Health Service Indian Hospital in Tuba City. One of the most surprising findings was the pattern of heavy and intermittent drinking of young males, which included withdrawal symptoms that indicated alcohol dependence, who, by the time they reached their late 30s and 40s, were abstinent or had controlled drinking, with or without treatment. This longitudinal pattern calls into question the more common description of alcoholism as a lifelong disease. The researchers' findings also reveals that solitary drinkers were less likely to be abstinent or have controlled drinking 25 years later. Women who were in trouble with alcohol appeared to be labeled as deviant and to be open to sexual exploitation.

Within the Navajo community, Kunitz and Levy found that people lacked knowledge of the deleterious effects of alcohol, including the effects on pregnant women. They also noted that until the era of World War II, most Navajo lived in remote areas with bad roads, little transportation, and little involvement with the cash economy. This meant that alcohol was not very accessible. By the 1940s, many Navajo had access to more reliable transportation and had the cash to afford to drink.

Solitary Drinking

> "No more. That's all." On her feet again to pour her second drink,
> Mrs. Lethwes firmly makes this resolution, speaking out loud since
> there is no one to be surprised by that. But a little later she finds
> herself rooting beneath underclothes in a bedroom drawer, and
> finding there another bottle of Gordon's and pouring some and add-
> ing water from a bathroom tap. (Trevor 1996:192)

In this fictional story, the unhappy Mrs. Lethwes continues to drink
prodigious amounts of gin throughout the day, as she often does, until
she becomes unconscious by dinner time. The kind of solitary, secretive
drinking so vividly described by writer William Trevor is difficult to
find in the ethnographic literature. Is it that ethnographers, often
working in cultures not their own, are not privy to this kind of private
pain? It is interesting to note that Kunitz and Levy, in the research on
the Navajo cited above, found that solitary drinking was considered to
be *the* definition of problem drinking by the Navajo community.

Drinking in Moderation

Mark Keller (1979) found ample historical evidence that during
biblical times there were many intoxicated Jews, and for many centuries, the blessing over the wine began with a warning against drunkenness. But by the Middle Ages, drunkenness was no longer feared, and
moderate and controlled ritualized drinking became the norm. Today, a
population group that is often used as an example of people who are not
abstinent but have not had a widespread problem of alcohol dependence is Eastern European Jews. A prevailing explanation, as summa-
rized by Keller (1979), has been the use of wine in rituals that begin for
some at birth, where a baby boy is given a taste of wine during circum-
cision, and continues throughout life during religious observances and
celebrations such as the Shabbat (Friday evening prayers), Havdalah
(Saturday evening prayers), weddings, and Passover. It is possible that
in a culture where its young people have learned to drink as a part of
life, alcohol does not have any "taboo" appeal. Another explanation is
that drunkenness is seen as a characteristic of the out group (the Gen-
tiles or non-Jews).

Drink as Food

Barbara Gallatin Anderson (1979) observed wine drinking at family dinners in the Seine-et-Oise region of France in 1957–1959. During
that period of time the official statistics estimated that the average
French adult drank 23.78 quarts of wine in a year, while the average
American drank 9.29 quarts. According to Anderson, a key to this prodigious wine drinking was that the French viewed wine drinking as
being healthy. This perception was strengthened by effective advertis-

ing by the French wine lobby, which distributed desk blotters to schools that portrayed a liter of wine as being the equivalent of 850 grams of milk, or 370 grams of bread, or 5 eggs. The campaign also disparaged the drinking of water, and the phrase "water is for frogs" was posted on subway signs (Anderson 1979:431). Furthermore, the lack of good refrigeration made milk a dubious household choice. As they grew up, French children drank *eau rougie* (reddened water) from the age of two years on. This water with a couple of soup spoons of wine added, however, was not considered to be an alcoholic drink.

Alcoholic drinks may indeed have nutritional value. For example, African millet beer is a source of calcium, iron, and vitamins B and C (McElroy and Townsend, 2009:212), and the people recognize the beer as food. When people switch to "high prestige" imported beers, however, they lose important nutrients. Backstrand et al. (2001) conducted a study among pregnant and nonpregnant women, living in the Solís Valley in Mexico in the mid-1980s, who often consumed large amounts of pulque. The researchers found that pulque can be a good source of ascorbic acid, riboflavin, iron, and thiamin, which were nutrients that were relatively low in the women's diet. The authors caution that no matter how important these nutrients are, any alcohol can, in fact, have adverse effects on the fetus.

COSTS OF ALCOHOL ABUSE

In the United States, alcohol use and drunken comportment incur heavy costs. The National Institute on Alcohol Abuse and Alcoholism (NIAAA) estimates that alcohol use is involved in approximately 60% of fatal burn injuries, drownings, and homicides; 50% of severe trauma injuries and sexual assaults; and 40% of fatal motor vehicle crashes, suicides, and fatal falls. In addition, heavy drinkers have a greater risk of liver disease, heart disease, sleep disorders, depression, stroke, bleeding from the stomach, sexually transmitted infections from unsafe sex, and several types of cancer. Alcohol use disorders affect approximately 18 million people in the United States (http://rethinkingdrinking.niaaa.nih.gov/).

In a car-dominated culture such as that of the United States, drinking and driving is a major concern. According to the National Highway Traffic Safety Administration in 2002, 41% of people who died in car accidents had a blood alcohol concentration of greater than zero (driver or pedestrian in a pedestrian fatality) and 35% were fatal accidents involving driver or pedestrian with a BAC of .08 or higher (Hingson and Winter 2003:63). The alcohol-related fatalities were not evenly distributed among population groups in the United States. For example, 68%

of the traffic fatalities of Native Americans involved alcohol, in comparison with 50% of the traffic fatalities of Mexican Americans, 38% and 39% of traffic fatalities of whites and African Americans, 24% of the traffic fatalities of Cubans, and 19% of the traffic fatalities of Asian Americans and Pacific Islanders (Hingson and Winter 2003:65).

ALCOHOL AND HOMELESSNESS

So entwined are homelessness and alcohol abuse that, in parts of the world, the same word is used to describe both conditions. In Finland, for example, the word *puliukko* (referring to an elderly man who drinks lacquer) was used for homeless people (Glasser 1994) and in Quebec the word *robineux* (a French form of the word for rubbing alcohol) was used as a synonym for homeless (Glasser, Fournier, and Costopoulos 1999).

The prevalence of alcohol abuse and dependence within the homeless community ranges from 30% to 70%, depending on the criteria for alcohol abuse and dependence that is used (Glasser 2002). Alcohol use can be both a cause and an effect of homelessness. Alcohol use can eat up a person's finances as well as contribute to job loss, poor health, and strained family relationships, which can cause a person to lose housing. Once homeless, it is difficult for an individual to focus on substance abuse treatment when basic survival needs for food and shelter are barely met. The stress and danger associated with homelessness also may feed back into the cycle of relying on alcohol or other substances as a coping strategy.

James Spradley (1970), an anthropologist working in the skid row of Seattle during the 1960s (discussed in chapter 1), found that the intermittently employed men living on skid row used alcohol as a source of camaraderie. Here alcohol was an adaptation to life on the streets as well as a cause of becoming an "urban nomad." Often members of skid row were incarcerated for intoxication for a month. When they came back to the streets, they often became drunk again. When asked about it, one of Spradley's community consultants told him the feeling among the men after a month without a drink was "you owe yourself a drunk," which became the title of Spradley's well-known book.

COLLEGE DRINKING

Alcohol use and misuse has long been associated with the college experience. Why students drink and what they think about drinking are fundamental to understanding college drinking. Yet, according to

Quintero and colleagues (2005), there is little research that explores these questions. In a small qualitative study of 59 Hispanic college students attending a state university in the US Southwest, the researchers asked the students to list all of the positive and negative attributes of alcohol use. The lists were then tabulated for the most frequent answers, which were grouped into various themes. The researchers found that the most salient positive attributes associated with drinking were: socializing, fun, relaxation, distraction (i.e., an escape from one's problems), it feels good, and makes people more talkative (Quintero et al. 2005:298). The most salient negative attributes associated with drinking were: drinking and driving, makes people violent, accidents and injuries, hurting someone or yourself, and headaches and hangovers (Quintero et al. 2005:301). When the research team asked the students to discuss the reduction of risk of drinking and driving, the students said they used the designated driver. Their interpretation of the driver's use of alcohol, however, should be noted: for some of the students, the designated driver drank *less* than the people riding in the car but did not abstain altogether. As one student said, "as a designated driver he felt comfortable getting a 'buzz' but had to avoid getting 'hammered' because of his driving responsibilities" (Quintero et al. 2005:302). This is the type of qualitative research that can help inform prevention of dangerous drinking on campuses.

It was fortuitous that Michael Moffat (1989) was conducting his ethnography of college dorm life in the early- and mid-1980s when the drinking age, which had been 18, was raised to 21. Moffat was living in

a dorm and posing as a full-time undergraduate student to gain an insider's perspective of college culture. As an anthropologist, Moffat primarily listened and participated in dorm life. When he began his participant observation in 1977, the keg party was a centerpiece of communal life on each floor of the dorm. When the drinking age was raised and most of the undergraduates could no longer drink publically, Moffat observed how the scheming to circumvent the new rules became a bonding activity in itself. He documents how dorm rooms were cleared of furniture so that 30 guests, the limit at the time for people in a room, could be crammed in. There was an understanding at the time that the no-drinking rule referred to *public* behavior, but that what occurred behind the door of one's room was *private* and sacred (Moffat 1989).

College binge drinking (i.e., consuming five or more drinks in a row for men and four or more in a row for women) is a serious problem on many college campuses throughout the United States. It has many repercussions: its toll on the health of the students (including alcohol poisoning and traffic fatalities), academic failure of its students, damage to property on and off campus, assaults, sexual assaults, and the deterioration of living conditions for all students due to intrusions such as excessive noise and vomit in the communal living spaces.

A great deal of data on binge drinking emanated from the College Alcohol Study, undertaken by the Harvard School of Public Health, which began in 1992 and ended after 14 years. A total of almost 50,000 randomly selected students at 140 colleges in the United States participated in the study (Wechsler and Nelson 2008; Wechsler n.d.). Among the most salient findings were:

- A total of 44% of students taking this survey drank four or more drinks in a row (for women) or five or more drinks in a row (for men) during the past two weeks, and this rate was stable throughout the years of the study.
- Over the course of the years of the study, there was an increase in both the number of frequent binge drinkers (three or more times during the past two weeks) as well as the number of abstainers.
- The drinking style of almost half of the students that reported any drinking is drinking to get drunk.
- Student binge drinkers tend to be male, white, and under 24 years of age.
- The strongest predictor of binge drinking is fraternity or sorority residence or membership.
- The students least likely to binge are African American or Asian, age 24 years or older, or married.
- Frequent bingers are more likely to miss a class, vandalize property, and get hurt or injured as a result of their drinking.

A pertinent question to ask is whether binge drinking is "deviant" on college campuses or is a cultural norm? This distinction is an important one to make according to Karen Leppel (2006) because if binging is deviant, then increasing the bonds to nonbinging campus networks would help students reduce their alcohol intake. On the other hand, if binge drinking is the norm, then one would try to change the culture itself. This potentially can occur through the encouragement of more nonalcohol focused activities or promoting moderate drinking for those who are of the legal age to drink. However, the student leadership for culture change away from binge drinking is, by definition, an always shifting cadre of people as students graduate.

In my classes, students discuss what they see as some college rules that may have the unintended consequences of *increasing* drinking rather than decreasing it. For example, before students go to a campus event that they know will include a bag check for alcohol, some drink as much as possible (and drink high-alcohol-content drinks such as vodka) so they are high prior to arriving at the event. This is called *pregaming* by the students, which college counselors point to as a cause for alcohol poisoning.

CULTURE AND DRINKING

In reviewing the ethnographic record of alcohol use in much of the world, Marshall hypothesized about the relationship between culture and drinking behavior, which is in need of further testing. Below I reproduce five of Marshall's conclusions that are useful in understanding the cultural beliefs and practices surrounding drinking:

Selection of vodkas in Russian liquor store.

- Solitary, addictive, pathological drinking behavior does not occur to any significant extent in small-scale traditional, pre-industrial societies; such behavior appears to be a concomitant of complex, modern, industrialized societies.

- When members of a society have had sufficient time to develop a widely shared set of beliefs and values pertaining to drinking and drunkenness, the consequences of alcohol consumption are not usually disruptive for most persons in that society. On the other hand, where beverage alcohol has been introduced within the past century and such a set of beliefs and values has not been developed completely, social—and sometimes physiologi-cal—problems with ethanol commonly result.

- All societies recognize permissible alterations in behavior from normal, sober comportment when alcoholic beverages are con-sumed, but these alterations are always "within limits." The limits for drunken comportment usually are more lax than those prescribed for sober persons in the same situations.

- People who lacked alcoholic beverages aboriginally borrowed styles of drunken comportment along with the beverages from those who introduced them to alcohol.

- When alcoholic beverages are defined culturally as a food and/ or a medicine, drunkenness seldom is disruptive or antisocial. (Marshall 1979a:451–456)

In an excellent review of the link between anthropology (including archeology and historical anthropology) and alcohol, Dietler (2006) notes that as a topic of inquiry, alcohol use can lead to an understand-ing of identity, power, trade, and economics in prehistory (before writ-ten history). Historically, alcohol had an important role in colonization in Africa and in the New World. Contemporarily, looking at alcohol use can be crucial to understanding the construction of identity and role and power distribution within the household, within communities, between women and men, and between socially distinctive groups. Finally, alcohol use (as well as abstinence) is central to many religious practices and religious changes throughout the world.

CONCLUSION

Alcohol has been called the "embodied material culture" in that it is the kind of material culture that *is created to be destroyed* through ingestion into the body (Dietler 2006). As we have seen, alcohol use, pro-duction, introduction, and effects have been studied in depth cross-cul-turally. The ethnographic literature provides insights into how people view alcoholic drinks, which may be seen as food, as a sacred food for the gods, or as an excuse to act outside the bounds of behavior viewed as normal. Drinking may be perceived as a community-building activity or as socially disruptive, and at times has both effects in the same culture. How people learn to drink and how they learn to act while drinking varies widely, not only from culture to culture, but also at different times in a group's history. In the next chapter we look at the cross-cultural ethnographic literature regarding tobacco, which, unlike alcohol, traveled from indigenous North America to Europe and beyond.

EXPERIENTIAL LEARNING ACTIVITIES

- Interview an international student on campus to learn about the drinking *cultures* in his or her country. There are usually many cultures within a country, and this conversation is most meaningful when the international student can discuss the cultures of which he or she is a part and knows best. Prepare open-ended questions about the occasions when a person drinks. What happens at and after these occasions? How does the drinking behavior vary by gender, religion, rural/urban living, social class, the presence of public transportation, and perhaps other factors? What is the international student's own drinking culture? Has it changed since he or she came to the United States? Will the student go back to his or her previous drinking styles (which could include abstinence) after returning home? What about drinking on a US college campus surprises or shocks the international student? For this interview to be successful there must be a level of trust and confidentiality. Students should create culturally appropriate pseudonyms in their written report on this assignment. International students in the class should choose an interviewee from a country and culture other than his or her own.

- If you are involved in university living, you have an insider's knowledge of university culture. Describe the drinking *cultures* within your university. Describe any harmful drinking practices that you have observed (e.g., drinking games) and harmful consequences you have observed (e.g., furniture broken, ambulances having to be called for alcohol poisoning, students flunking out due to missed classes). Based on your knowledge of this culture, design a campaign to target and reduce harmful drinking that you think addresses student culture. Consult with the professional staff within the counseling center of student services, which may offer useful statistics on the rate and types of dangerous drinking and negative consequences on your campus. The professional staff also may be able to point to activities that diminish the likelihood of harmful drinking (often referred to as protective factors), such as sponsoring alcohol-free activities on campus or promoting student interest in special activities such as art or volunteer activities.

Edward S. Curtis photograph of a member of the Arikara Nation with seven calumets (ceremonial pipes).

Chapter Three

Tobacco and Its
Global Reach

Tobacco, divine, rare, superexcellent tobacco, which goes far beyond all panaceas, potable gold, and philosopher's stones, a sovereign remedy to all diseases. . . . But, as it is commonly abused by most men, which take it as tinkers do ale, 'tis a plague, a mischief, a violent purger of goods, limb, health, hellish, devilish, out damned tobacco, the ruin and overthrow of body and soul. (Robert Burton, 1621, as quoted in Goodman 1994:17)

Robert Burton, a scholar who lived in the late-16th and early-17th centuries in England, wrote the above words in a medical textbook, *The Anatomy of Melancholy.* As the single most preventable cause of death in the United States (CDC *Tobacco Use* 2009), tobacco use presents a fascinating case of a legal substance with lethal consequences. As the quote above suggests, even early in the diffusion of tobacco from the New World to Europe and beyond, tobacco was recognized for both its euphoric qualities and the power and harm it held over individuals dependent on it.

INDIGENOUS USES

The tobacco plant is at least 8,000 years old and was known to the Amerindians of the southern and northern New World (Goodman 1994). This earliest known use we term indigenous use. Jacques Cartier noted St. Lawrence Iroquoians smoking tobacco in pipes made of stone or wood in his visits of 1535–1536 (von Gernet 2000). Tobacco was cultivated in the New World wherever it could grow, even among hunters and gatherers, such as the Haida and the Tlinglit of the Northwest Coast, who did not plant any other crop (Goodman 1994).

Tobacco may come from a Guarani word from precontact Haiti referring to the implement that was used to inhale the smoke (Ernst 1889). Drawing from printed documents from Spain from 1535, Dr. Adolfo Ernst, writing in *The American Anthropologist* summarizes the implement:

> It is a small tube in the shape of a letter Y. The stem was thrust into the smoke of the burning herb, the branches were put to the nostrils and, after repeated inhalations, a state of intoxication was produced, which lasted for some time. This implement . . . they called *tabco*, adding expressly that such was not the name of the herb, as some people believed. (Ernst 1889:133)

According to the historian Jordan Goodman, tobacco, which in its indigenous form had greater nicotine content than the tobacco in modern-day cigarettes, was used to induce hallucinations in shamans for their curing rituals. One such curing ceremony involved blowing smoke over the sick person in order to find the source of the illness. Once the source was located, the shaman extracted the foreign body by symbolically sucking it out with a straw.

European observers of tobacco use in Native North America compared tobacco to wine in its ability to induce dizziness, inebriation, and loss of reason (von Gernet 2000). Some Amerindians were seen having pipes in their mouths most of the day. In this way the indigenous use of tobacco was for both ritual as well as what we would call recreational use. Von Gernet observed what he calls "democratized shamanism"—everybody has the opportunity to connect with the spirits. He suggests that these Amerindians were nicotine dependent while they experienced a dream state and oneness with the spirit world.

There are still many traditional uses of tobacco in modern Native North American communities. Tobacco is smoked during a healing ceremony, may be sprinkled around the house for protection, may be a part of burnt offerings, or may be offered as a gift to others (Rhoades et al. 2000). A contemporary pan-Indian ritual is the use of the Sacred Pipe, which is filled with tobacco and smoked communally to emphasize the relationships between people (Paper 2007). The following describes elements of this ceremonial experience:

> When the pipe is lit, preferably with a coal or a smoldering braid of sweetgrass, a puff is offered to each of the Four Directions, Sky and Earth, and possible other spirits. Either before or after the pipe is lit, it is offered stem first to the spiritual recipients while prayers are said, whether spoken or silent. The pipe is then passed around the congregants in a sunwise direction.

The ritual creates a double communion. By offering tobacco smoke in a vessel from which both the offerer and the recipient both smoke, the smoke creates a communion between the spirits and the person. Second, as the pipe circulates around the circle from which all smoke, it creates a communion among the smokers. This is how the Sacred Pipe can make relationships not only with the spirits but the humans. Thus, strangers on sharing the Sacred Pipe become relations, no long enemies. (Paper 2007:154)

DIFFUSION OF TOBACCO AND SMOKING

From the time Columbus was offered a bunch of dried leaves as a present in 1492, to the widespread pipe smoking of sailors in the 16th century and the manufacture of pipes in England in 1570, smoking tobacco spread throughout the world (Goodman 1994; Norton 2008). Cigarettes, in contrast to pipes, became popular after 1845 when the French began manufacturing the South and Central American *papelate*, which was crushed smoking tobacco wrapped in vegetable matter such as banana skin or bark. The French renamed the papelate the *cigarette* and the wrapping was eventually made of paper. The widespread use of cigarettes did not occur until the 20th century with the advent of the automatic cigarette manufacturing machine and the extensive use of advertising (Samet 2000).

Europeans were impressed with the potential healing properties of tobacco through their contact with the Amerindians. The Spanish physician and botanist Nicolas Monardes (1493–1588) read firsthand accounts of the smoking of tobacco and identified what he called "nicotine therapy." He wrote of tobacco's ability to alleviate hunger and thirst and its ability to expel excess moisture from the body (Goodman 1994).

Innovations are most often adopted when the culture receiving the innovation is compatible in some ways with the innovation (Rogers 1995). Tobacco was adopted by Europeans at least in part because it was compatible with humoral medicine, which explained health in terms of a balance between the body's qualities of hot, cold, wet, and dry (Norton 2008; McElroy and Townsend 2009). Tobacco was thought to be hot and dry and could therefore restore health to a person who was suffering from a wet or cold malady (Goodman 1994). Thus, tobacco use became integrated with the already existing constructs of humoral medicine.

An example of the diffusion of tobacco comes from the work of Mac Marshall (2005), who traced the introduction of tobacco to the Caroline Islands of Micronesia. The cultures that form the Federated States of Micronesia (FSM) did not use any psychoactive substance before contact with the outside world. Tobacco was the first substance that was adopted in the late-17th century, having been brought to Guam and then to

Micronesia by the Spanish colonizers. The first word for tobacco in Micronesia was *suupwa*, which derives from the Spanish word *chupar*, to suck, in reference to the process of smoking large Spanish cigars. Marshall reports that the tobacco plant thrived in the Chuuk State of FSM by the 19th century. It was not until 1948 that commercially manufactured cigarettes were available in the Caroline Islands. Today, the tobacco farms of North and South Carolina ship tobacco to the Caroline Islands.

An important reason for the diffusion of tobacco is the tremendous profits that can be made from its sale, as well as the taxes that can be levied on tobacco. In 1988, the profit margin on cigarettes in the United States was 35% in contrast to other manufacturing profits, in which 10% was considered good (McGill 1988). Further, the taxes on tobacco products are also significant. For example, according to the Food and Agriculture Organization of the United Nations, the US tobacco tax revenue in 1986 was $9.4 billion (Goodman 1994). In the developing world, tax revenue on cigarettes can be a significant part of the total revenue.

As public health warnings about the dangers of smoking were being disseminated and taken seriously in the United States beginning in the 1970s, transnational cigarette corporations began to search for new markets for their products in the developing world. In a 1995 study of cigarette smoking in Namoluk, in the Chuuk State of FSM, 47% of the men and 6% of the women smoked, a gender difference that is often seen in the developing world where women are discouraged from smoking and drinking. This difference between rates of smoking between men and women parallels differences in sex roles that have translated into social norms: women are less powerful and rebellious than men, although the social norms that have traditionally kept women from smoking are diminishing (Pathania 2011). Women are also active in Micronesian churches, which generally discourage drinking and smoking.

Tobacco is thought of as a comestible (something edible) along with food and drink. On Namoluk, a person "drinks" a cigarette (*wún tamak*) and the belief is that this should be shared with others as with other food and drink. Marshall observes:

> When cigarettes are plentiful, those who have them will give single cigarettes to others to smoke by themselves. As supplies become limited between calls by trading vessels, smokers will share their remaining tobacco by passing a cigarette around among a group of men, each taking a deep draw before handing it to the next person. (Marshall 2005:373)

The leading causes of death in Micronesia are cardiovascular disease, cancer, stroke, and acute and chronic respiratory diseases that are all linked to cigarette smoking (Marshall 2005). Public health campaigns against smoking, according to Marshall, need to challenge the positive associations that cigarettes have within the culture.

HEALTH CONSEQUENCES

Wayne McLaren, who portrayed the rugged "Marlboro Man" in cigarette ads but became an anti-smoking crusader after developing lung cancer, has died, aged 51. . . . His mother said: "Some of his last words were 'take care of the children. Tobacco will kill you, and I am living proof of it.'" . . . Mr. McLaren, a rodeo rider, actor and Hollywood stuntman . . . was a pack-and-a-half-a-day smoker for about 25 years. In an interview last week, Mr. McLaren said his habit had "caught up with me. I've spent the last month of my life in an incubator and I'm telling you, it's just not worth it." (*Guardian*, 25 July 1992, as quoted in Goodman 1994:239)

According to the Centers for Disease Control, cigarette smoking is responsible for one in every five deaths in the United States. It causes more deaths each year than the deaths caused by HIV, illegal drug use, alcohol use, motor vehicle injuries, suicides, and murders *combined*. Further, smoking is responsible for 90% of all lung cancer deaths in men, 80% of all lung cancer deaths in women, and 90% of deaths from chronic obstructive lung disease. Compared with nonsmokers, smokers are at increased risk of heart disease and stroke, in addition to lung cancer and chronic obstructive lung disease (CDC 2010b).

The highest rate of tobacco use in the United States is among Native Americans and Native Alaskans with 42.6% using any tobacco products and 37.1% using cigarettes, in contrast to the general population rate of 31.5% for any tobacco products and 26.9% for cigarette use (Caraballo, Yee, Gfroerer, and Mirza 2008). Furthermore, 27.9% of Native American and Native Alaskan youth age 12 to 17 smoke cigarettes in contrast to 13.8% of youth in the general population who smoke (Caraballo et al. 2006). This means that new Native smokers are being recruited at a higher rate than their non-Native counterparts.

Contemporary Native Americans often consider tobacco to be both a sacred plant that deserves respect as well as a killer (Samet 2000). For example, in a prison with a high percentage of Native Americans, tobacco is used in ceremonies meant to conquer addiction to drugs, alcohol, and even cigarette smoking. Paradoxically, when used in small amounts for ceremonial purposes, tobacco may serve positive purposes, as it appeared to do in precontact times. It is likely, however, that the shamans who ingested great amounts of nicotine did in fact suffer and die (Winter 2000). One approach to reducing Native American smoking is to advocate the ceremonial use of small amounts of tobacco grown in the wild (Samet 2000), while discouraging tobacco's recreational use.

CIGARETTES AS CURRENCY

Very portable and immediately consumable, cigarettes are ideal for currency and have been used in a variety of circumstances where cash is not available, such as among soldiers and prisoners (Lankenau 2001). Stephen Lankenau (2001) conducted a study of the use of cigarettes as a commodity in US prisons after the smoking bans, which began in the 1980s. He led a team that looked at the factors that promoted the underground economy of cigarettes in prisons and found a very active and lucrative black market in cigarettes, which *increased* after the smoking bans were established. The activity depended on the ecology of the prisons (the older prisons had more unsupervised spaces), the inventiveness of the prisoners in hiding cigarettes and smoke, the complicity of the prison personnel in facilitating the black market, and the attitude of the prison staff in enforcing no-smoking rules. Cigarettes entered the prison via visitors, through prisoners on work release, and from prison personnel involved in the black market. One prisoner said he was able to send $500 to his girlfriend each week based on his participation in such an underground economy. Another prisoner in the study said:

> I would've never messed with coke on the street if I knew how much money I could've made selling cigarettes in the joint. (Lankenau 2001:158–159)

Prison wardens and jail administrators reported a decrease in illegal drugs entering their facilities since cigarettes were in such demand by the prisoners and so much money could be made through such trade.

The smoking ban in prisons was generally not accompanied by any smoking cessation aids, such as nicotine replacement therapy (e.g., a transdermal patch) or counseling or support, and prisoners were expected to quit on their own. In my own work with homeless populations (Glasser and Zywiak 2003), I have been told by recently released prisoners who quit smoking or cut down in prison how they were very disappointed in themselves for returning to smoking upon release. Having no help in smoking cessation or relapse prevention in prison means little support and skill development for not returning to smoking upon release.

In my ethnographic work in soup kitchens and homeless shelters, I have noted that, as in prisons, cigarettes take on a form of currency as well as being a medium for sociability (Glasser 1988). People ask each other for cigarettes, and this kind of exchange is part of the generalized reciprocity. One homeless man told me that even if he did quit smoking, he would keep some cigarettes on him in order to have something to give to people in exchange for something else. This use of cigarettes as barter is important to acknowledge, since it may be a hidden deterrent to quitting.

BELIEFS ABOUT SMOKING

In order to understand what people believe about smoking, one avenue of study is the focus group, wherein a small group of people are asked open-ended questions by a trained facilitator. The groups promote frank and informal discussion in order to explore a topic. The transcripts are analyzed, usually by more than one person, to identify underlying themes.

A prime example of focus groups was research that sought to understand the behaviors and beliefs of African American adults regarding menthol cigarettes, which are heavily marketed in African American communities (Richter, Beistle, Pederson, and O'Hegarty 2008). Although African Americans do not smoke more than other ethnic groups in the United States (Caraballo et al. 2008), they do suffer more serious tobacco-related illnesses than other groups. Among the findings of the focus group study was that African Americans viewed those who smoked nonmentholated cigarettes to be more "hard-core" smokers than those who smoked mentholated cigarettes. The participants in the groups thought that mentholated cigarettes were less harmful, even though this is not supported by research, and that one way to quit smoking would be to switch to nonmentholated cigarettes, whose harshness would be a deterrent to smoking. The participants were very aware that the tobacco industry heavily markets mentholated cigarettes in African American neighborhoods, such as on billboard signs and in print media. The participants described advertisements for nonmentholated cigarettes directed to the white community as featuring outdoor scenes, adventures, and athletics; they described the advertisements for mentholated cigarettes as emphasizing being relaxed, "kicked back," and cool.

CAMARADERIE AND SMOKING

A little understood phenomenon is the existence of camaraderie among smokers, which has become more pronounced as smoking is relegated to designated areas and the smoking population decreases. In an ethnography of a psychiatric hospital in Norway, Skorpen, Anderssen, Oeye, and Bjelland (2008) discovered the meaning of the smoking room for the patients. By 1994 in Norway, smoking had become illegal inside public places and outside on public property; the prohibition applied to psychiatric institutions—that is, everyone except the patients. The outcome was the creation of a smoking room at the end of some of the wards. These smoking rooms became, in effect, patient-only oases, places where hospital staff were clearly unwelcome. Skorpen and colleagues (2008) document the mutual support and camaraderie found inside the smoking rooms.

The link between smoking and camaraderie has not been lost on the tobacco industry. In a study of internal tobacco industry documents, Anderson, Glantz, and Ling (2005) found that advertisements from the 1990s tended to show smokers and nonsmokers together, enjoying each other's company. The late-1960s Virginia Slims advertisement campaign "You've Come a Long Way, Baby," which stressed independence and strength, became "It's a Woman Thing" in the 1990s, which stressed women enjoying each other's company and being accepted by other women who were both smokers and nonsmokers. Similarly, the iconic 1960s Marlboro Man, alone on his horse, evolved to become amiable looking groups of cowboys enjoying a moment of relaxation. Again, the smokers and nonsmokers were comingling, implying that smokers are not being stigmatized by smoking. The smiling and sociable cowboy was a way for tobacco companies to appeal to a younger market—people interested in a sense of community in contrast to the lone cowboy.

SMOKING AND WOMEN

Smoking and gender is an important area of concern because of the possible complications for the pregnant woman, the fetus, and issues of secondhand smoke in the home. The Surgeon General's Report regarding smoking and reproductive health (CDC 2004) cites pregnancy complications, low birth-weight infants, premature births, stillbirths, and infant deaths among pregnant women who smoke. It is estimated that 12% to 22% of pregnant women smoke.

A qualitative study of 53 low-income pregnant smokers in the United States discovered that all of the women were aware of its dangers to their unborn child and made some attempts to either quit or cut down (Nichter, Nichter, and Muramoto et al. 2007). In addition to the two obvious groups—those who continued to smoke and those who quit—a third group emerged whom the authors call the "shifters": those women who made periodic attempts to quit or cut down intermittently throughout their pregnancy. Those who were able to quit (30%) were characterized as having a strong sense of identity as a mother. They had the most stable living arrangements (often living with their mothers), and they had people in their support network who encouraged them to quit, even if those people still smoked. The women who were able to reduce their smoking by at least 50% (43% of the women) felt that not quitting entirely made them a failure. The women in this study said that although their health care providers told them that it is bad to smoke when pregnant, they did not give them any actual practical advice on quitting. The women also said they had trouble controlling their environment in that they often lived with people who smoked. A strength of this study was that each woman was interviewed three times during the pregnancy by the same interviewer who saw them while they may have been trying to quit or cut down.

In traditional societies, smoking has been significantly associated with being male. What happens when a society becomes increasingly "modern"? A case in point is Vietnam, where currently the rate of female smoking is only 3.4% in contrast to a 50% rate for males. In this rapidly urbanizing country, however, there is concern that if women are not included in tobacco-use prevention campaigns and programs they may take up smoking, as has occurred in countries where traditional gender roles have changed.

In order to explore the meaning of smoking among women in Vietnam, Morrow, Ngoc, Hoang, and Trinh (2002) combined focus groups, surveys, and open-ended questions in research conducted on a sampling of over 2,000 young women age 15–24 who were workers and students in Ho Chi Minh City. The researchers found that the young women in the study did not have a clear idea of the health consequences of smoking, saying instead that smokers become "thin, pale and weak" (Morrow et al. 2002:685). The women said the reasons women smoke is because they are sad (*buon*) or bored (*chan*), two words that are linked in Vietnamese (Morrow et al. Trinh 2002). The authors recommend that the public health community make the health consequences of smoking clearer and that being sad and bored, which may indicate depression, may be a risk factor in smoking initiation. Among the steps for reducing initiation into smoking for women in Vietnam, the authors recommend that the health risks of smoking be presented in a clear and comprehensible manner and that community health workers help women who may need more assistance in addressing mental health problems such as depression.

SMOKING AND ADOLESCENTS

Developing Tobacco Dependence

The issue of adolescence and smoking is an important one in that adolescence is a time when many people are first introduced to smoking. More than half of adult smokers became regular smokers before the age of 18 (National Survey on Drug Use and Health 2009). Nicotine dependence in adults is measured through validated instruments such as the widely used Fagerström Tolerance Questionnaire (FTQ), which may not match the adolescent reality or worldview. The questions on the FTQ are (Fagerström and Schneider 1989; Heatherton, Kozlowski, Frecker, and Fagerström 1991):

- How soon after you wake up do you smoke your first cigarette?
- Do you find it difficult to refrain from smoking in places where it is forbidden?
- Which cigarette would you hate most to give up?
- How many cigarettes per day do you smoke?
- Do you smoke more frequently during the first hours after awakening than during the rest of the day?
- Do you smoke even if you are so ill that you are in bed most of the day?

Adolescents, who are still under their parents' and teachers' supervision and may not have the money to smoke a lot, may not score very high in cigarette dependence when asked the above questions. Nevertheless, they may still feel dependent on cigarettes.

What are adolescents' own views of their nicotine dependence? A qualitative study of 85 adolescents in British Columbia, Canada, revealed the adolescents' conceptualizations of what makes people dependent on smoking (Johnson, Bottorffa, Moffat et al. 2003). The ethnographic research uncovered adolescents' own emic categories for dependence, including:

- Being socially dependent on smoking in order to "fit in" with other youth
- Smoking for pleasure, including inhaling and exhaling smoke, handling cigarettes
- The empowering aspect of being able to smoke and to give out cigarettes (or not) to friends
- The emotional aspect in that some adolescents felt that smoking was a good form of stress relief
- Smoking could fill a void when there was nothing else to do, such as waiting at a bus stop
- Full-fledged dependence was being addicted to smoking and needing it to feel "normal"

Thus, even if adolescents may be considered light or irregular smokers by some measures, by their own evaluation they may indeed be dependent on cigarettes (Johnson et al. 2003).

A qualitative study of Hispanic and American Indian youth in New Mexico sought to further uncover adolescents' reasons for initiating smoking and maintaining smoking (Quintero and Davis 2002). Mood management was a primary reason for smoking, as illustrated by these statements of Hispanic young women smokers:

> I stress about . . . my family and stuff like that. . . . When I'm all stressed out or like I'm about to explode, I just like, I'll get a cigarette, and I'll be relaxing all good. (Quintero and Davis 2002:447)

> It . . . gives you a buzz. . . . It like drowns all of your worries. (Quintero and Davis 2002:447)

Another salient reason for smoking was image maintenance, or ways to project a "cool" and "mature" identity. An American Indian young woman smoker remarked:

> I think it was because a lot of people thought you'd be all popular if you smoked. It would make you feel older, make you feel like you're gown up. (Quintero and Davis 2002:449)

One of the youth in the study provided a subtle observation of the meaning of smoking for some youth, which the authors summarize:

> Popular, "normal" youths smoke in order to provide a visible cue, a relatively penalty-free way of demonstrating that they are "cool" without having to indulge in more risky, less socially acceptable, and less visible activities like drug and alcohol use. (Quintero and Davis 2002:449)

The American Indian youth of the Quintero and Davis study appear to be especially sensitive to the addictive aspects of smoking, perhaps because of the historical role of alcohol abuse within the Native communities. One young American Indian woman commented:

> I just think I need it. Right now I'm addicted. I want to get away from it. Every time they pull out a cigarette, I must want to have one or something. (Quintero and Davis 2002:449)

Another young American Indian woman commented on what she thought about young men smoking:

> If I see a guy and he's like addicted to smoking, then it kind of gets sick. I don't want him to have the smell and everything. . . . It's like they're going to put more attention to the cigarettes more than you. (Quintero and Davis 2002:450–451)

Quintero and Davis suggest that smoking prevention and cessation efforts should focus on these culturally nuanced reasons for smoking among youth. The role of the heavy and targeted tobacco advertising to youth was not brought up by the youth, and a heightened awareness of the financial resources that the tobacco companies bring to bear in order to entice smoking among youth could be further explored.

Smoking as Play

In their search for why young people who have been brought up learning about the health risks of smoking can turn to smoking when entering college, Stromberg, Nichter and Nichter (2007) analyze the various ways that cigarettes are used as a kind of "play" by college students. The researchers specifically sought out college students who smoked 20 cigarettes or fewer per week and interviewed them between one and five times over the course of their freshman year. These were young people who, for the most part, did not identify themselves as smokers; rather, they were smoking to provide structure within what they considered to be ambiguous situations. The authors related this "filling in of time" to theories of children's play. Through play, children learn roles, methods of interaction with others, acceptable and unacceptable behavior, as well as other practices that pertain to their culture; their play is patterned after something meaningful in their culture.

For example, smoking at parties is a way to facilitate social interaction and is also a way to look like you are "doing something" in moments when you are not talking with another person:

> Everybody that goes to a party is always there just to like, not to just sit there and watch people—you're there to kick back and meet people and socialize. Everybody always wants to fit in . . . and the best part of a party is always outside and you can't just go out and do nothing, so usually you smoke. (Stromberg et al. 2007:8)

> If I saw someone at a party, or a group of people, that were smoking I'd ask them for a smoke. And that would get me into the conversation or get me closer or something. It's a tool. . . . (Stromberg et al. 2007:8)

> I smoke [at a party] to look comfortable when I feel out of place or don't know any people, or maybe more out of boredom. If I am in a situation where I didn't know a lot of people it would be because I didn't have anything better to do. Smoking a cigarette makes me look like I'm doing something. (Stromberg et al. 2007:9)

Although the students in this study did not consider themselves "serious smokers," some did advance during the course of the year to buying their own cigarettes and smoking by themselves. This was most often explained as a way to relieve stress or boredom. Considering how addictive nicotine is, we can hypothesize that a percentage of these low-level smokers will become regular smokers.

CIGARETTE MARKETING STRATEGIES

Since the percentage of the population in the United States who smoke has dropped by 50% since 1965 (Rodu and Cole 2007), tobacco companies have been searching for inventive ways to recruit new smokers. The tobacco companies' marketing strategies depend on analyzing the cultures of the people who are most vulnerable to beginning or continuing to smoke. A major target of tobacco marketing is youth. The advocacy group Campaign for Tobacco-Free Kids (http://www.tobaccofreekids.org) has identified the following as some of the techniques that are used by tobacco companies in their marketing of youth:

- Advertise tobacco products in convenience stores near schools and playgrounds using large signs that are visible from the street
- Suggest that smoking can satisfy an adolescent's need to be popular, feel attractive, and manage stress
- Use price promotional ads that are popular with teens
- Promote flavored cigarettes that appeal to youth

Tobacco companies also have engaged in antitobacco campaigns; however, studies suggest that their methods, such as the Philip Morris "Think, Don't Smoke" television campaign that ran for 12 months, are *ineffective* (Wakefield et al. 2006). "The greater the teenagers' potential exposure to the ads, the stronger their intention to smoke and the greater their likelihood of having smoked in the past 30 days" ("When Don't Smoke Means Do" 2006). Moreover, the Philip Morris campaign directed to parents, "Talk. They'll Listen" appears to ignore the tendency for youth to listen to their peers, not their parents. The Lorillard Tobacco Company television advertisement "Tobacco is Whacko if You're a Teen" implies that smoking is inappropriate for teenagers, but not unhealthy for others. It frames smoking as an adult activity, which may make smoking even more attractive to teens. The conclusion of the research on antismoking advertising by tobacco companies is that youth end up with more positive attitudes toward the tobacco companies for sponsoring the advertisements and there is no evidence they are effective in preventing youth from smoking.

Indonesia is a country where tobacco companies are powerful and where tobacco taxes contributed approximately 10% of the government's revenue in 2002 (Nichter et al. 2009). It is a country where 62% of the men smoke, although only 1% to 3% of the women smoke. Tobacco advertising is highly innovative and takes into account many of the cultural values of the people. One of these values is the control of emotions. Smoking is considered a way to deflect negative emotions successfully. Much of the smoking is of the indigenous cigarettes, *kreteks*, which are a blend of cloves, tobacco, and hundreds of additives. Kreteks are inhaled deeply and are considered to be an even worse health risk than conventional cigarettes smoked in the West (Nichter et al. 2009).

A popular brand of cigarette in Indonesia is the Djarum L.A. Lights. In the advertisement below, in order to deal with an angry girlfriend, the young man is able to transform her hostile words ("bla bla bla") by smoking L.A. Lights so that her words become "la la la." A countermarketing strategy would involve discussions with young people about how knowledge of their culture is being used to sell this high health-risk product.

In the 1990s in the US, tobacco companies were one of the first businesses to advertise in lesbian, gay, bisexual, and transgender (LGBT) communities as well as offer philanthropy to the LGBT community (Smith, Thomson, Offen, and Malone 2008). The LGBT market is considered profitable for tobacco companies since the rate of smoking in these communities is significantly higher than in the population as a whole. When Smith and colleagues conducted focus groups within the LGBT communities in four US cities, they were surprised to learn that a dominant theme to emerge was that these communities felt they had "arrived" in that they were finally visible to marketers. The targeted marketing indicated social acceptability and recognition of their economic power. The LGBT community in this research also did not perceive smoking as a gay health issue.

Other groups that are vulnerable to encouragement to smoke are homeless and populations suffering from a mental illness.[1] In the United States, approximately 70% of adults who are homeless smoke (Zerger 2009) and approximately 41% of those identified as mentally ill smoke (Lasser, Boyd, and Woolhandler et al. 2000). The tobacco industry has identified both of these communities as significant parts of their "downscale" customers (Apollonio and Malone 2005). In a study of approximately 400 internal tobacco industry documents that referred to the homeless, mentally ill, homeless organizations, and psychiatric institutions, Apollonio and Malone (2005) wanted to discover the details of the marketing to this population and found a variety of ways the tobacco industry used their knowledge of the culture of homeless and mentally ill populations to promote smoking to these vulnerable populations. Such strategies include:

- Donating cigarette brand labeled blankets to homeless shelters
- Donating free cigarettes to homeless shelters, soup kitchens, and mental health services

- Trying to enlist homeless advocacy groups, with varying success, in resisting smoking restrictions inside shelters for staff and clients
- Making donations to homeless veterans events and selling cigarettes at these events

The link between mental illness and cigarettes can also be explained historically, as cigarettes were at times used as rewards in the era of state-administered mental hospitals, before the deinstitutionalization of the mentally ill in the 1970s. I recall my own days of social work training when people inside the psychiatric hospital were rewarded with cigarettes at regular cigarette breaks during the day. If one was not a smoker before hospitalization, it would have been tempting to become one, since cigarettes took on so much prominence. I recall patients continually asking me if I had a "butt" since they were willing to smoke the ends of the cigarettes that most smokers threw away.

Thus, understanding culture can be powerful and effective as tobacco companies search for ways to encourage dependency. A countermarketing strategy is to make this use of culture *explicit* to the communities that are being manipulated.

UNINTENDED CONSEQUENCES OF SMOKING BANS

An interesting area of research is discovering the unintended consequences of public policy, which, although meant to improve the quality of life, may have the opposite effect for some members of the community. California prohibited smoking inside bars in 1998. Moore, Annechino, and Lee (2009) conducted a series of qualitative studies between 2001 and 2007 in order to discover the law's impact on the bar customers, employees, and neighborhoods around the bars. A key to the methodology of the studies was observations of bars and follow-up interviews. A total of 390 bars were observed a minimum of three times each. A few of the bars provided patios or other designated places for the smokers, but typically the streets outside of the bars became the main site for smokers. Some of the unintended consequences for leaving the bar to smoke on the street were the safety concerns, especially of the women customers and workers who were now spending time on the street. It was awkward for female bartenders who might have to discipline male patrons and then encounter them on the street in a less-controlled environment than inside the bar. Women who were often poor who lived in the vicinity of the bars had to deal with the noise and secondhand smoke created by the smokers on the street. On the positive side, Moore, Annechino and Lee (2009) uncovered a sense of solidarity among the women smokers, which could lead to an increase in social support.

CONCLUSION

Tobacco moved from the New World to Europe and far beyond due to its euphoric effects, its high liability for physical dependence, and its great profitability. Today, profitability motivates its aggressive marketing. Despite tobacco's implication in death and disease, it a legal drug. In the next chapter we turn to the case of drugs, which presents us with wide variations in cultural practices, both in the use of drugs and in their legality.

EXPERIENTIAL LEARNING ACTIVITIES

- Interview an "elder" in your family or community and ask him or her to identify changes in the smoking and other forms of nicotine use that he or she has witnessed in their lifetime. The person can consider the advertisements, for example, for various brands of cigarettes and the impact these had on him or her growing up. Or the family member might recall the time when everyone could smoke anywhere and even the doctor might have smoked during a medical visit. Perhaps your interviewee witnessed these changes as a process over time, or because he or she moved or became a member of various subcultures. For this assignment, define an "elder" as being 50 years old or more.

- Design a public health campaign for a particular cultural community that addresses prevention of or quitting tobacco use. Gather knowledge of the important characteristics of the community through readings, focus groups, interviews, and participant observation. Ask a group within the community to design literature or billboards that will touch a responsive chord in the community. In the example of two billboard designs discussed in chapter 5 (see p. 91), we had asked members of the community what would influence them and their neighbors not to begin smoking or to quit if they were smoking. Many women in the Hartford billboard campaign said that staying healthy for their children or grandchildren would motivate them to not smoke and to not permit smoking in their own homes. Discuss how billboards located on buildings and in view of hundreds of pedestrians each day can be culturally sensitive to an urban and poor population.

Note

[1] There is a wide variation in the meaning of mental illness as used by researchers. A mental illness may be diagnosed or undiagnosed, acute or chronic, mild or severe, related to drugs, alcohol, or medical conditions, or not.

Chapter Four

Drug Use and Drug Prohibitions

Like alcohol and tobacco, drugs have been used for a wide variety of social, religious, and medicinal purposes. Drugs also have been the target of prohibitions, depending on the era, the place, and oftentimes the characteristics of the drug users. When we look at the effects of drugs on humans, we must also consider both the impact of the drugs (legal and illegal) themselves and, with regard to illegal drugs, the adverse consequences of law enforcement and incarceration.

Anthropologists have studied drug use worldwide using archeological evidence, historical documents, and ethnographic explorations. In this chapter we will examine anthropological perspectives on drug use in indigenous cultures, research spurred by HIV prevention, and the controversies regarding law enforcement and incarceration. Discussions identify a sample of the anthropological research regarding a selection of drugs, including hallucinogenic mushrooms, peyote, coca leaves, ayahuasca, morphine, heroin, khat, marijuana, ecstasy, methamphetamine, prescription drugs, cocaine, and illy.

INDIGENOUS USES OF MIND-ALTERING DRUGS: THE CASE OF HALLUCINOGENIC MUSHROOMS, PEYOTE, COCA LEAVES, AND AYAHUASCA

J. Bryan Page (2004) hypothesized that humans may have accidentally learned that ingesting plants can remedy illness or induce altered states of consciousness in the course of foraging for food. Examples of evidence of the use of hallucinogenic mushrooms are found in chronicles written by the Spanish conquerors of Mexico. Spaniards loathed Native religious rituals associated with *teonanacatl*, the Nahuatl name for mushrooms that means "flesh of the gods." The Spanish cleric Fray Bernardino de Sahagún, writing in the mid-1500s, said that those who ate the mushrooms "see visions, feel a faintness of heart and are provoked to lust" (Furst 1990[1972]:7). There is also archeological evidence of "mushroom stones," which were stones comprised of an upright stem with a manlike or animal face that was crowned with an umbrella- shaped top (Furst 1990[1972]. These mushroom stones were found in Guatemala and southeastern Mexico that date to 300–500 BCE and on frescoes found in central Mexico that date from the year 300 CE.

Dr. Francisco Hernández, a physician to the King of Spain, writing in 1651, wrote of the hallucinogenic mushroom, the *teyhuintli*, noting that it caused

> not death but a madness that on occasion is lasting, of which the symptom is a kind of uncontrolled laughter . . . these are deep yellow, acrid and of a not displeasing freshness. There are others again which, without inducing laughter, bring before the eye all sorts of things, such as wars, and the likeness of demons. Yet others there are not less desired by princes for their festivals and banquets, and these fetch a high price. With night-long vigils are they sought, awesome and terrifying. (Furst 1990[1972]:9)

Two examples of drug use within contemporary indigenous communities are peyote and coca leaves.

Peyote is a small, spineless cactus in which the principal active ingredient is mescaline. Mescaline can also be produced through chemical synthesis. Peyote is a hallucinogen that can cause profound distortions in a person's perception of reality. Under the influence of hallucinogens, people see images, hear sounds, and feel sensations that seem real but are not (NIDA 2009a). Peyote appears to have been used in precontact times among the native people of Mexico. It then diffused to native peoples in the United States in the late 1800s, as a part of a revitalization movement that rejected infidelity, gambling, and alcohol and favored a direct communication with God (Grobsmith 1981).

In an ethnography of the Lakota Sioux Rosebud reservation of 1981, Elizabeth Grobsmith (1981) recounts the history of peyote use among Native Americans. The Peyote Cult, now called the Native American Church, came to the Rosebud Reservation in South Dakota in the 1920s. According to the Native American Church, peyote clears the mind and allows God's spirit to enter the individual. It is used for expanding one's consciousness and for healing (Jones 2007). During a peyote ceremony Grobsmith (1981) observed the singing of songs, accompanied by passing around a rattle and a drum to all of the participants. At this point peyote, a bitter-tasting cactus button that contains the hallucinogen mescaline, is passed around and eaten in the form of a paste and a tea. Although it makes people feel very nauseated, they rarely excuse themselves from the meeting. To alleviate the discomfort, each person holds a tin can into which he retches. . . . The hallucinogenic properties of peyote enable participants to have revelations that are cures or answers to their prayers. (Grobsmith 1981:81)

Peyote is an illegal drug in the United States. Because of its ceremonial and religious role, however, its use is now permitted in the chartered churches of the Native American Church in North America (Grobsmith 1981).

There is evidence that the sharing of coca leaves and the invocation of the deities had been done for thousands of years before the Spanish conquest (Allen 2002). The description below was written by anthropologist Catherine Allen, as she participated in the funeral of Rufina, a 44-year-old Quechua woman in Peru who died giving birth to her 13th child.

Hallpakusunchis, Taytáy ("Let us chew coca together, Father") he said.

Luis [Rufina's husband] accepted with thanks. He blew over the *k'intu* [small offerings of coca leaves] before putting it in his mouth, calling quietly on *Pacha*, the Earth; on *Tirakuna*, the Places; and on *Machula Aulanchis*, the Old Grandfathers. (Allen 2002:4)

Within the Peruvian village where Allen lived in 1976–1977 and often visited afterward, the effect of chewing coca leaves appeared comparable to drinking a cup of coffee and taking an aspirin. Allen points to the usefulness of coca leaves for the vitamins and minerals in them that are needed by people living in a climate where few green vegetables grow and who exist on a heavily carbohydrate diet. From the Quechua point of view, coca is thought of as a "hot" substance that counters the "cold" of a staple food, such as potato, and is used to achieve an equilibrium based on humoral medicine (Allen 2002). In the United States coca leaves are a Schedule II drug.

Cocaine was isolated from the coca leaf in Germany in 1860 and was thought of as a wonder drug, an anesthetic, a cure for opium addiction, and a tonic. Coca cola was made with cocaine until 1906 (Singer 2006a). In the United States cocaine was classified as a narcotic in 1922, and both cocaine and coca leaves were banned from import (Allen 2002). Eventually this ban diffused to Peru where the transporting of coca leaves is now prohibited. Although the ban is aimed at the *narcotraficantes* involved in processing the coca leaves into cocaine, the effect of the ban has been to restrict the sale and transportation of coca leaves for the people who have used it traditionally. According to Allen, people of the Andes have substituted alcohol and cigarettes, items that do not have the same ritual meanings as

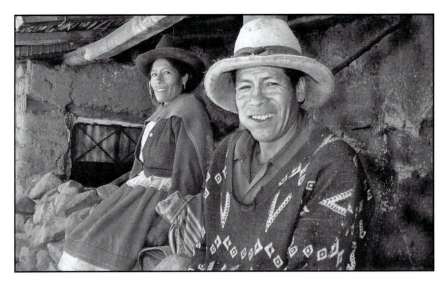

Quechua couple chewing coca.

coca leaves, for the web of sharing that was once dominated by coca leaves (Allen 2002).

In a fascinating exploration of how humans have strived to leave the physical world and enter into an altered reality or altered states of consciousness, Lynne Hume, in *Portals: Opening Doorways to Other Realities Through the Senses* (2007), documents how visual symbols, sound, dance, touch, smells, and drugs have been and are used to aid in achieving the ability to experience what is "beyond the door" of every-day reality. Hume employs the word *entheogen*, which literally means "the god within," for psychoactive substances.

An example of an entheogen is ayahuasca, which is a Quechuan term for a South American brew that often combines tobacco with the plants *Brugmansia* and *Datura* (species names) (Hume 2007). This brew induces vomiting as well as complex visual and mind-altering effects. After using the brew, people report emotions ranging from bliss, elation, horror, fear, and, at times, sensations of love. In indigenous communities in the Amazon, Hume reports that ayahuasca is used for medicinal purposes. The *cuarandero* (healer) drinks the brew in order to learn the patient's problem and be led to the cure.

There are also inherent dangers associated with the use of aya-huasca. For example, some people who come to South America in search of a spiritual quest have had the following experience:

> Eager tourists are generally provided with accommodation as well
> as the ayahuasca. After long journeys up the Amazon in the com-
> pany of other tourists from different parts of the world, they are

usually each offered a toilet roll and a vomit bowl, and then assist-
ed in their spiritual journey via the ayahuasca "sacrament." Accompanied by shamans singing chants, blowing smoke and
camphor into the air, and rattling for most of the night, they invariably experience discomfort, nausea and powerful visions that
might change their lives. (Saunders, Saunders and Pauli 2000, as
cited by Hume 2007:134–135)

Hume cites more permanent negative consequences, including psy-
chotic episodes and severe depression among these Westerners. Even
taking ayahuasca in an appropriate ritual context by indigenous people
does not guarantee a positive experience. Mind-altering drugs can also
exacerbate previously unknown mental problems in some people.

Sara Lewis (2008) describes the ayahuasca-induced psychological
crisis experienced by some Westerners who want to experience the lim-
inal (transitional) state that is observed in people who work with a traditional shaman in seeking spiritual growth. This liminality is seen as
a necessary stage that exists between the individual's old and new self.
Liminality often occurs during *a rite de passage* (initiation rite) when a
person has separated from his or her previous identity but has not yet
become integrated with the new one (see Turner 1969). Lewis terms the
distress that ayahuasca causes Westerners as "spiritual emergencies"
and suggests that this occurs because they have no cultural road maps
for their experience and feel very isolated.

DRUG LAWS AS CULTURAL ARTIFACTS: THE CASE OF MORPHINE, HEROIN, KHAT, AND MARIJUANA

From 1880 to the present, people of the United States and Europe
began what Page calls "western moralism," which was and is a movement "to protect people from ruining themselves through drugs" (Page
2004:376). This movement toward the prohibition and criminalization
of drugs occurred at the same time the United States was becoming
more ethnically diverse. Page suggests that it is no wonder the focus of
this criminalization initially was on opium, which was smoked by Chinese immigrants who first came to America in the early 19th century
to find work.

In the United States, the 1914 Harrison Narcotic Act required
anyone who sold or distributed narcotics (including pharmacists and
physicians) to register with the federal government. Among the lasting
effects of the Harrison Narcotic Act are the criminalization of drug
addicts and a flourishing black market for drugs that are sold at greatly
inflated prices (Mignon et al. 2009). A further significant development
in the history of drug control in the United States was the 1970 US Con-

trolled Substances Act. This law regulates drugs, and it created categories, called schedules of drugs, which we reviewed in the first chapter.

Despite the efforts to control drug use through law enforcement, drug use in the United States is widespread. In 2008, according to the Centers for Disease Control, 8% of the US population reported using an illicit drug (marijuana/hashish, cocaine including crack, heroin, hallucinogens, inhalants, or any prescription-type psychotherapeutic drug used nonmedically) in the previous month (National Center for Health Statistics 2011).

In recounting the history of morphine (and later of heroin), Merrill Singer offers an excellent example of the changing attitudes toward these drugs and laws created to regulate them, which appear to be dependent on the demographic composition of the community of users (Singer 2006b). Morphine, whose name derives from Morpheus, the Greek god of dreams and sleep and is made from opium, was discovered in laboratory experiments conducted in the early 1800s. It was more potent than raw opium and was soon used as a painkiller by practitioners of Western Biomedicine. This use continues today. Opium itself had been used in the ancient Middle East for approximately 6,000 years and was sold over the counter in the United States throughout the 18th and 19th centuries. It is likely that regular opium users became physically dependent on it but did not suffer the social consequences that people do today since it was legal.

Morphine was used as a painkiller throughout the Civil War, where it was administered to wounded soldiers by the newly invented hypodermic needle. After the Civil War, many people became dependent on the drug, thereby giving it the name "soldier's disease" in reference to the withdrawal symptoms of these newly morphine-dependent people. Estimates suggest that as many as half a million people were then suffering from this iatrogenic disease, which is a disease that comes about because of medical treatment (Singer 2006b). During this time, grocery stores and pharmacies sold patent medicines containing opiates, and one could have opiates delivered from Sears and Roebuck by mail order (Mignon et al. 2009).

Heroin, whose name derives from the feeling of being heroic, was developed in 1898 by the Bayer Company as a cure for morphine addiction as well as a cure for respiratory illnesses (Singer 2006b). Initially heroin was thought to be nonaddictive and was heavily advertised throughout Europe and the United States. By 1914 its addictive properties were known and it was outlawed in the United States. It then went underground. Those addicted included users from the era when heroin was legal, as well as new users. The 2010 National Survey on Drug Use and Health of the US Department of Health and Human Services estimates that there are currently 359,000 individuals who are heroin dependent or abusive in the US.

Khat is a stimulant drug that is derived from a flowering shrub native to East Africa and the Arabian Peninsula. The fresh leaves and shoots of the khat plant are chewed and then retained in the cheek until all of the juices are extracted. Khat became known in the United States with the migration of people from Somalia, Ethiopia, and Yemen.

According to the US Drug Enforcement Administration, chewing khat is an established cultural tradition for many social situations in the areas of primary cultivation: East Africa and the Arabian Peninsula. Several million people may currently be using khat worldwide. The largest concentrations of users are in the regions surrounding the Middle East (http://www.justice.gov/dea/concern/khat.html). Khat is legal in much of Europe, East Africa, and the Arabian Peninsula. Khat is classified as a Schedule I drug in the United States due to the presence of one of its chemical constituents, cathionone (NIDA 2011).

In a review of the medical and epidemiological research on khat, Manghi and colleagues (2009) found that khat is an integral part of life in the populations in which it is used. Use covers the spectrum from socially beneficial in its community-building characteristics to harmful in terms of its propensity to cause people to neglect obligations and to become physically dependent on it. The authors found it analogous to alcohol, whose use also includes a range of outcomes. Medically, the effects of khat use can be psychological dysfunction, gastrointestinal problems, periodontal problems, cancer, low birth weight if used by pregnant women, and cardiovascular problems. Manghi and colleagues (2009) nevertheless found evidence of khat's socially integrative functions, as the following description of a khat session from Yemen suggests:

> For organized khat sessions, participants may carefully be screened and receive an invitation from their host, who also provides the khat. Those taking part in the session, and the amount and quality of the khat reflect the status of the host. Those invited to such incidental khat sessions are expected to organize similar events in their turn. . . . Such organized sessions may include different festivities, feasts, and rituals held in association with births, circumcisions, and marriages. (Manghi et al. 2009:5)

In addition to being a part of the fabric of life, khat affects the economy of Somalia and Yemen, as it is both a producer of income for those who cultivate it and a drain on a family's budget for those who use it.

Khat presents a challenging case of a drug that is viewed very differently as its users cross borders in their international diaspora. Unlike peyote, which, it can be argued, is used for religious purposes, khat's use appears to be social and recreational. Since khat users may not be aware of its possibly deleterious effects, they might benefit from culturally congruent health education.

In the early part of the 21st century in the United States, perhaps no drug engenders as much political debate as marijuana. In an excellent history of the change of marijuana from a legal to an illegal drug, Singer documents how marijuana (along with opiates and cocaine) was a part of the quotidian life since colonial times in the United States (Singer 2006a). Marijuana was most often used as an elixir and was a patent medicine. It was a widely recommended drug prior to the Civil War. In addition to being prescribed as a treatment for pain, it was prescribed for over 100 different illnesses including alcoholism. The daily dosages were significant, equaling what a current illicit user consumes in a month (Singer 2006a). Antimarijuana sentiment started in the early part of the 20th century, as its use became associated with large numbers of Mexican and Mexican-American migrant workers in the west, who were thought to be violent due to their marijuana use.

In the 1960s and 1970s, marijuana use was widespread among the middle class, especially among the youth. By 1971, 51% of college students said they had tried marijuana (Singer 2006a). The folk wisdom became that marijuana was the "gateway" drug, meaning that once a person used marijuana, he or she would be inextricably drawn to using harder drugs, such as heroin. The hypothesis is based on the theory that although most drug users have used alcohol and tobacco first, marijuana is the first *illegal* drug that most youth use. The evidence, however, is that only a small fraction of those who use marijuana go on to harder drug use (Singer 2006a).

The effect on the respiratory system of regularly smoking marijuana is similar to the effect of smoking tobacco (NIDA 2010c). Nevertheless, marijuana is seen as a potentially useful drug for stimulating the appetite, controlling nausea and vomiting following anticancer therapy, moderating neurological and movement disorders, relieving certain types of pain, and decreasing intraocular pressure associated with glaucoma. Currently there are 14 states in which it is legal to use marijuana for medical purposes. Although marijuana is still classified as a Schedule I drug (see chapter 1), patients who use marijuana and doctors who prescribe it are now exempt from prosecution in those states where it is legal for medical use (Dresser 2009).

The tension between the legalization of medical marijuana and its continued illegal classification is illustrated by a report of violence against growers of marijuana in the State of Washington where marijuana is decriminalized. The growers of medical marijuana, who also distribute it, are targets of robberies and confront thieves who have no qualms about injuring or even killing them (Yardley 2010). These growers are known to cultivate large quantities of marijuana, whose value is tied to the fact that it is still illegal. In practice it appears that the cultivation and distribution of marijuana, even for medical use, is not well regulated. Moreover, the line between "medical" use and "recreational" use is not clear to law enforcement authorities who consequently have little sympathy for growers.

There is also a debate among those who would like marijuana *decriminalized* (criminal penalties for its cultivation and sale but no penalty for possession of small amounts) versus those who would like it *legalized* (allowing the cultivation, sale, and use of marijuana). What would the effect of either of these paths be on the levels of abuse or dependence? Arguments for marijuana's legalization include being able to implement quality control, being able to enforce laws regarding age of consumption, eliminating the large marijuana black market, saving individuals and families the destruction incarceration brings, and not making a mockery of a law that is so routinely ignored. There are arguments for keeping the laws against marijuana in place due to marijuana's harmful effects (see NIDA 2010c for a summary). Arguments against legalization include the possibility of marijuana being marketed to children and adolescents as is done with tobacco (see "Room for Debate Blog: If Marijuana is Legal, Will Addiction Rise?" *New York Times* July 19, 2009).

Despite the intense debate that marijuana fosters, there is a surprising paucity of research on marijuana's medical efficacy, which may be attributed to the political and ideological debates surrounding it and to the difficulty researchers have experienced in obtaining marijuana for their studies (Cohen 2009).

EFFECT OF LAW ENFORCEMENT AND INCARCERATION

The US System

One might ask, how effective are the drug laws? Since 1972, in the United States there has been a fivefold increase in the number of people arrested for nonviolent drug-related crimes *without* a comparable decrease in crime or in drug use (Moore and Elkavich 2008). The increase in the rate of incarceration is sometimes cited as an indication of the success of the War on Drugs (the Nixon administration initiative to define and reduce illegal drug trade), ignoring the impact of incarceration on the individual, his or her family, or the community. The increased rate of incarceration has resulted from tougher drug laws, less judicial discretion in terms of sentencing, and greater policing efforts.

In a review of the current knowledge about drug use, arrests, and incarceration, Moore and Elkavich point out that the rates of illicit drug use are about the same among African Americans and whites (7.2% and 7.4%) and are lower among Latinos (6.4%). Given that whites make up a greater proportion of the US population than African Americans, whites are about 72% of all illicit drugs users and African

Americans are 15% of all users (Moore and Elkavich 2008). African Americans and Latinos, however, are approximately 60% of the incarcerated population. This discrepancy is due in part to greater policing efforts in neighborhoods populated by people of color. In Illinois, an African American man is 57 times more likely than a white man to be incarcerated for a drug offense (Lurigio and Loose 2008).

Most incarcerated individuals are from urban areas, while most prisons are located in rural areas, far from the prisoners' homes and families. Prisons are a boon for rural communities for the jobs they provide. Thus, there is an economic incentive to maintain or grow prison populations; whole regions are dependent on an "industry," which is dependent on prosecuting people for committing crimes, including those that are drug related. Furthermore, prisons swell the population of a rural area since the US Census counts prisoners as a part of the population based on where they are situated at the time of the census. Counting prisoners as residents of otherwise sparsely populated districts gives those districts the minimum population requirement to elect a representative to the state senate. Elected officials of the districts that house prisons do not tend to represent the prisoners' interests (Richburg 2009). Thus, these communities benefit from people who use illegal drugs and from tough drug laws. Although prisoners are politically "included" while in prison, ironically, after prison, those with drug-related arrests are often excluded from public housing and federal assistance for college (Moore and Elkavich 2008).

Moore and Elkavich attribute much of the disparity between who is actually *using* drugs versus who is *doing time* for drugs to the great gulf between those in power, including the researchers and scientists whose work contributes to social policy, and the people and their families affected by incarceration. Without any personal connection to communities affected by unequal policing, strict drug laws, and imprisonment without rehabilitation, policy makers continue to imprison nonviolent drug offenders from poor African American and Latino communities.

International Drug Trade

The effects of law enforcement's efforts to stop drug use are felt around the world, as the people in developing countries are often the producers of the raw materials involved in the drug trade. In an insightful overview of the drug trade and of law enforcement to prevent it, Singer (2008) documents how the appetite for the drugs in the industrialized nations fuels this international drug trade. From the poppy fields in Afghanistan to the coca fields of Bolivia, farmers are caught between their economic survival and the web of the drug cartels. The evidence is that international interdiction and attempts at eradicating the plants used to make illegal drugs have had very little positive impact on curtailing the drug trade because fields that are destroyed

Destruction of poppy fields by locals in Farah Province, Afghanistan.

can easily be replaced; that is, the plants are grown somewhere else. Furthermore, interdiction has involved funding local antidrug military and law enforcement groups, who mete out harsh punishments—and at times human rights abuses—to growers and others suspected of being involved (Singer 2008).

Drug Policies and HIV

At the time of the 18th International AIDS Conference in the summer of 2010, evidence pointed to disastrous consequences of the 50-year-old international War on Drugs, especially its effect on HIV prevention (Wood et al. 2010). The delegates attending the 2010 AIDS conference created the Vienna Declaration, a plea for decriminalizing drug use, increasing evidence-based drug treatment (i.e., treatment practices for which there is systematic empirical evidence of the treatment's effectiveness), and basing drug policy on scientific evidence (Vienna Declaration 2010). In areas like Eastern Europe and Central Asia, where HIV is spreading rapidly, injection drug use accounts for as much as 70% of cases of HIV. Policies affecting injection drug users have a significant impact on the fight against AIDS.

Criminalizing drug use pushes drug users further underground and away from prevention and health care. Incarcerated drug users are further exposed to HIV in prisons. The billions of dollars spent on the War on Drugs could be spent on public health focused on the prevention of HIV. The global illicit drug market generated over $320 billion in 2003. This level of profit fuels crime, violence, and corruption and has destabilized countries including Colombia, Mexico, and Afghanistan (Vienna Declaration 2010).

ANTHROPOLOGICAL RESEARCH ON
CLUB DRUGS AND PRESCRIPTION DRUGS

Club Drugs

Club drugs are the category of drugs that include MDMA (ecstasy), methamphetamine, GHB (Gamma hydroxybutyrate), Rohypnol, ketamine, and LSD (http://www.nida.nih.gov/drugpages/clubdrugs.html). They are so named because they tend to be used by teenagers and young adults within the setting of bars, nightclubs, dance parties (raves), and concerts. Different club drugs have different effects. In the case of ecstasy, which acts as both a stimulant and a hallucinogen, people may take it in order to have enough energy to keep dancing or partying all night or for a feeling of emotional warmth and a general sense of well-being. Club drugs can also produce anxiety, chills, sweating, teeth clenching, muscle cramping, sleep disturbances, depression, impaired memory, hyperthermia, and addiction.

In the US, methamphetamine (meth) comes from foreign or domestic superlabs or from small, illegal labs erected in houses, apartments, hotel rooms, or outdoors. Meth can be made using a variety of chemicals that are harmful. Not only does the end-product cause harm (to the central nervous system of the user), but the chemicals in the recipe also contaminate the environment (Methamphetamine Laboratories n.d.). Meth increases the release of dopamine in the brain, resulting in feelings of intense euphoria. Chronic meth abuse causes reduced motor skills and impaired verbal learning, as well as emotional and cognitive problems (NIDA 2010e).

Ketamine distorts perception and can cause sensations ranging from a pleasant feeling to feelings of detachment. In high doses it can cause delirium and amnesia. Because it is odorless and tasteless, people who want to commit a sexual assault can put it in an unsuspecting victim's drink, without the victim detecting it. The drug GHB has a tendency to produce feelings of euphoria and sociability. It can cause drowsiness, nausea, headaches disorientation, loss of coordination, memory loss, unconsciousness, seizures, and comas (NIDA 2010b). Like ketamine, GHB can be added to drinks without detection.

Anthropological research on club drugs has tried to gain an insider point of view of the meaning and consequences of club drug use from the users, usually through in-depth interviews. In a review of the literature of the international research on club drugs and the dance scene, Hunt, Moloney, and Evans (2009) found that participants see these events and drug use at them as essentially harmless. The rave attendees feel the events promote a sense of community, as youth from different social-class backgrounds come together and blend on the dance floor. The dancing, the music, and the drugs work together to create a sense of oneness for all participants (Hunt et al. 2009).

In a study of polydrug use among ecstasy users, Boeri and colleagues (2008) interviewed 94 out-of-treatment youth (ages 18–25) who had used ecstasy four times within the previous three months. They found that, along with ecstasy, all had used alcohol, 79.8% had used nicotine, 85.1% had used marijuana, 40.4% had used methamphetamine, 38.3% had used hallucinogens, 34% had used powder cocaine, 34% had used unprescribed pills, and 25.5% had used unprescribed opiates (Boeri, Sterk, Bahora, and Elifson 2008). (The term unprescribed means that a prescription is required to obtain the medication/drug/pills, but the person in possession of them does not have a prescription for them or is taking the medication that was prescribed for himself or herself in a manner or dosage other than what was prescribed. Nonprescription medication/drugs/pills do not require a prescription to obtain them and are sold over the counter.)

The authors found three distinct patterns of polydrug use: separate, synergistic, and indiscriminate. In the pattern of *separate use*, ecstasy and other drugs were not used on the same occasion. For example, a young woman described her ecstasy and methamphetamine use this way:

> Ecstasy, I feel like I can do that maybe once a month or maybe even less than that because it's fun but it's an intense experience. And doing meth is really intense, but it's something you can do every day too, it's a very functional drug. (Boeri et al. 2008:526)

In *synergistic use*, the combined drug use was during the same drug event and the drugs were used for an enhanced effect or as the individual was coming off of a high. For example, one young person said:

> Alcohol doesn't make [ecstasy] last longer, but it makes it more exciting. (Boeri et al. 2008:528)

In the *indiscriminate-use* pattern, the individual used ecstasy and whatever other drug was available. Some described doing this to get "totally messed up" and "have a good time" while others in this pattern described ending up in the emergency room.

The fact that polydrug use was so prevalent in this study, and included licit (e.g., alcohol, nicotine) and illicit (e.g., marijuana, methamphetamine) drugs, led the authors to recommend that drug research, harm reduction programs, and drug treatment initiatives reflect the reality of polydrug use.

In an ethnographic exploration of methamphetamine use in the US rural South, Sexton, and colleagues (2006) conducted in-depth interviews with 34 active, not-in-treatment methamphetamine users in rural Kentucky and Arkansas. In this study, the users themselves made the methamphetamine from locally available materials (e.g., ingredients found in cold tablets, fertilizer, camera batteries) based on widely circulated recipes. Methamphetamine was smoked, injected, snorted, and swallowed. Some of the smokers used aluminum foil in the shape of boats. The methamphetamine was placed in this boat, a flame was held below it, and the vapors were inhaled through a straw or other implement (Sexton, Carlson, Leukefeld, and Booth 2006).

The participants in this study talked about the boredom of rural life, peer pressure, unemployment, and widespread availability as reasons for ongoing use. They liked the euphoria, increased interest in sex, and feelings of energy and efficiency. Participants also described their adverse reactions to methamphetamine, including their increased tolerance (needing more of the drug to get the same effect), the paranoia they saw in their friends, and weight loss. The authors suggest that methamphetamine prevention programs tailored to rural US populations discuss the adverse reactions based on the narratives of rural methamphetamine users.

Prescription Drugs

As described earlier, prescription medication drug abuse means taking a prescription medication that is not prescribed for the individual (unprescribed), or taking it for reasons or in dosages not prescribed. The commonly abused classes of prescription drugs include opiates (e.g., Vicodin and OxyContin), CNS depressants (e.g., Valium, Xanax), and stimulants (e.g., Dexedrine, Adderall) (NIDA 2005). The health consequences of prescription drug misuse are serious and can be fatal. The opiates and depressants can become addictive and produce physical dependence (NIDA 2005).

The rise in prescription drug misuse can be attributed to the significant increases of the number of prescriptions written in the United States, their social acceptance, and the aggressive marketing of the pharmaceutical companies (Volkow 2008). The number of deaths from prescription opiates increased 160% in the five years between 1999 and 2004. The number of deaths from opiate painkillers outnumbered the total deaths involving heroin and cocaine in 2006 (Volkow 2008). This is a complex issue; prescription medications are central to healing and alleviating human suffering.

Taking unprescribed medications or prescribed medications in dosages that are not intended is a growing trend among teens and college students. The 2004 Monitoring the Future Survey of College Students and Adults estimates that 7.4% of college students used Vicodin without a prescription. According to findings from the Harvard School of Public Health Alcohol Study, which surveyed 10,904 students in 2001, students who abused prescription stimulants had higher levels of cigarette smoking, heavy drinking, risky driving, and marijuana, MDMA (ecstasy), and cocaine use (Whitten 2006).

In an exploratory study of the culture surrounding prescription drug misuse, Quintero, Peterson, and Young (2006) interviewed 52 college students at a public university in the Southwest (United States). The authors found three major clusters of reasons for using these prescription medications that were obtained from family and friends: self-medication (for sleep, pain, and weight loss); socio-recreational (to feel "mellow" and relax); and academic functioning (to stay up to finish papers or cram for an exam). Student statements give us a flavor of their rationales:

> I was up really late doing homework and I had been drinking coffee [because] I had wanted to get a paper done, so I was staying up drinking coffee, and then I just took a Klonopin so that I could fall asleep.

> I guess I just like to do kind of the opiate based drugs that, I don't know, make you feel real mellow and relaxed and . . . kind of disconnected in a way.

> Studying is doing drugs for a lot of people I know . . . it's bumping Adderall. 'Cuz Adderall makes you concentrate, and if you snort it, it's even more potent. (Quintero et al. 2006:911)

The students interviewed in this study did *not* tend to classify their prescription drug use as "drug use," as illustrated below:

> Most people in college aren't there to do drugs. They have to work hard and focus. The hard drugs will really mess you up.

> I think hard drugs are more dangerous and people know that. In terms of the kids that I know they just want to have a good time on the weekends and not think about work. (Quintero et al. 2006:911)

This emic view implies there is a perception among college students that prescription drugs are not as dangerous as "hard drugs" and using prescription drugs is not "drug use." Understanding students' perceptions is valuable in preparing prescription drug misuse prevention material, since students may feel that the words "drug use" do not pertain to them.

Perhaps the most surprising aspect of the Quintero, Peterson, and Young study is the confidence the students expressed about how to mix prescription drugs, both with each other and with alcohol. This is medically risky, but some of the students believed that, based on their and their family's and friends' experiences with prescriptions and what they could learn over the Internet, they were able to use many drugs without danger, as illustrated below:

> Well, recreationally, I would take Vicodin and I would take half of one to drink. When I get drunk I get kind of loud, and so when I take half of one I can still be functional, but be a little mellower and my body just feels looser and relaxed. (Quintero et al. 2006:920)

In reference to her Valium use, one female student told the researchers:

> If you have friends over or if you go out it's just a really great money saver because you take one and you have a beer, then you're pretty much good for the rest of the night, instead of buying like seven or eight beers or something. (Quintero et al. 2006:920)

DRUG USE INITIATION AND CONTINUED
PARTICIPATION: THE CASE OF COCAINE

How are individuals initiated in drug use and the drug trade? Anthropologists have utilized the political economy explanatory model, which explores the relationship between individuals, governments, and markets. Earning money through the illegal drug trade has great allure for people with little power and economic prospects, given the great profits that can be made.

In 1985, anthropologist Philippe Bourgois moved into an apartment in East Harlem, New York, intending to study all manner of the underground economy. What he studied instead was the burgeoning crack business. Crack is the street name given to the form of cocaine that has been processed to make a rock crystal, which, when heated, produces vapors that are smoked. The term "crack" refers to the crackling sound produced by the rock as it is heated (NIDA 2010d). Bourgois was able to document the millions of dollars worth of illegal drugs sold outside his apartment. Although the majority of people in Bourgois' East Harlem neighborhood were not drug dealers, he paints the picture of the allure of this part of the underground economy, enabling people who are shut out of the mainstream economy by their poor education, generations of racism, and neighborhood segregation to earn a living to support themselves and their families, and to earn the respect of their peers. As one of Bourgois' participants, Felix, told him:

> Hell, yeah I felt good when I owned the Game Room [crack house]. In those days everybody be looking for me; everybody needed me. When I drove up, people be opening the door for me, and offering to wash my car. Even kids too little to understand anything about drugs looked up to me. (Bourgois 2008:77)

In spite of Felix's experience, Bourgois concluded that, given the vagaries of the crack trade, people made very little money from selling crack at the street level.

Many studies of participation in drug use and the drug trade have focused on men. Claire Sterk (1999) documented the lives of women in Atlanta, Georgia, who were regular users of crack cocaine and were not in treatment. She found that most of the women in her four-year study began their drug use in high school, within their circle of friends. In addition to tobacco and alcohol, they used marijuana, heroin, cocaine, or crack cocaine.

> Alice, a slender, thirty-two-year-old African American woman, was very content with her life until she started using drugs. She was sixteen at the time. When I met her, she was in her late twenties and

an injection drug user. By then, she also had an eleven-year-old son and a two-year-old daughter. Her older sister was taking care of the children to allow Alice to focus on some changes she wanted to make in her life. . . . The last time I spoke with Alice, she was worried about AIDS. She had been losing weight and had learned that a man with whom she had had sex and injected drugs several years before had died of AIDS. (Sterk 1999:1, 2)

A pattern that Sterk found was that at first a young woman's circle of friends included both drug users and nonusers, but if she continued using drugs, her friends became exclusively users. Soon the young woman had an identity as a drug user. Many of the women described their escalating use of crack, from what they considered to be controlled use to wanting to be high all the time.

Smoking crack hits you right away, and you keep chasing that first high. It's a drug that lets you get high only one time. The next time it doesn't feel as good, and you just chase a feeling. Chasing makes it so you can't control your habit. (Sterk 1999:43)

Once dependent on crack, the women in Sterk's study obtained money from jobs (if they could keep them), financial assistance, and the drug trade itself. Among the "aristocracy" of the drug world were women who called themselves "queens of the scene" because of the respect they garnered. These were women who could cook powdered cocaine into rocks of crack or were high-level dealers; they also tended to regulate their crack use so they could still concentrate on their cooking.

Other women participated in theft and sex work in order to earn the money for crack. One group of women Sterk followed were the older ones, in their thirties and forties, who, for the first time in their lives, became involved in drugs and crime. The impetus appeared to be a crisis in their lives such as the breakup of a long-term relationship. The following narrative of one of the older women in Sterk's study reveals the disappointment she felt:

I can't tell you about it. I'm at a place where I thought I'd never be. For years I fought against becoming a bad person. . . . I can't even look at myself anymore. . . . I hadn't had sex for a long time and here I am acting like a whore. (Sterk 1999:76)

Another ethnographic exploration of drug use is Kojo Dei's study (2002) of 16–21-year-olds in an African American and Jamaican community within the outer ring of New York City. Dei is especially interested in the attitudes of the youths' parents, since most of the drug use appeared to be done indoors in the youths' own home. The primary drugs used were marijuana, cocaine, crack, heroin, and angel dust (a common name for PCP). Dei found that the adults of the community were more focused on the lack of jobs, lack of recreation for the youths, poor housing, harassment by the police, and unresponsive politicians than on youth drug use. The parents also recognized the change in attitude toward drugs in the community once the neighborhood became predominantly African American and Jamaican. Community members told Dei that when organized crime controlled the drug trade and when the community was predominantly white, the police turned a blind eye to drug use and drug traffic. The parents were also more concerned about the effects of alcohol than drugs in their community. Dei found a wide range of drug involvement, from total abstinence to occasional use to dependence. He also discovered that the abstinent youths were still friends with the youths who were using, and the users were not socially ostracized from the community.

ETHNOGRAPHY OF SUFFERING: THE CASE OF HEROIN AND INJECTION DRUG USE

The realities of living as an injection drug user have been vividly portrayed in the ethnographic works of Singer (2006b) and Bourgois and Schonberg (2009). Singer followed Tony, a pseudonym for a heroin addict with whom Singer conducted a life history based on interviews with him over a seven-year period of time. Tony was recruited into the world of heroin by his father who was addicted to morphine after being injured in the Korean War (an example of an iatrogenic illness, i.e., one produced by medical treatment). Tony's life was filled with thefts, shootings, gangs, drugs, and prison. He told Singer about his relationship with heroin:

> Heroin. Straight heroin. It's like it runs through my veins. You know, you can have a girlfriend with dope, it's like your wife. . . . It's like it calls to me. . . . It's like I am in love with it. I'm in love with heroin more than I am with a woman. I give everything to heroin. (Singer 2006b:46)

By the end of their seven years together, Tony, currently in his 40s, appeared to be filled with regret. He had been incarcerated eight times, had not been able to keep a girlfriend, had become HIV positive, and appeared to be exhausted by his life that had been filled with violence and crime. Tony told Singer:

> To be honest, I don't even know where I am at with my health right now. I just finished medications for walking pneumonia and they want me to go back. It's the same spots from before. But I keep procrastinating. I seem to have this smoker's cough that I never had before. I have the virus [HIV] but my T-cells ain't come down yet enough to get medication. The last time I was tested was seven

months ago. And with the hepatitis my enzymes are not too bad. . . .
I think that my viral load is up there, but I am scared to find out if
it is enough to start the medication. That means you are on your
way [toward dying]. (Singer 2006b:139)

In over ten years of observation, Philippe Bourgois and Jeff Schonberg (2009) came to know and photograph heroin injectors who were
homeless and living in alleys, cars, trucks, tents, and factories in a
warehouse and shipyard district near San Francisco. Their written and
photographic ethnography, *Righteous Dopefiend*, is especially graphic
regarding the toll on the human body and spirit of living in filthy sur-
roundings while injecting heroin into any vein possible. As clandestine
injection drug users who were constantly running from the police, they
were vulnerable to multiple and repeated infections that invaded their
bodies through the needles, cotton, and other paraphernalia they used
to administer the drugs.

When these injection drug users did seek medical care, it was in
an emergency. For example, a member of Bourgois and Schonberg's ethnographic team found one of their community consultants, Hogan,

listless and shivering with fever on his mattress in the mud behind
the Dockside Bar & Grill. A large abscess on his left leg had swollen
to the size of a grapefruit. Earlier that week, he had been denied ad-
mission to the emergency room and he was too debilitated to try
again. (Bourgois and Schonberg 2009:99)

Through the advocacy of the ethnographic team, Hogan was admit-
ted to the emergency room, where the staff found maggots in the wound.
He required a skin graft on his left calf. Within one week of the skin graft,
Hogan was discharged and quickly returned to his muddy encampment.

The challenge in focusing on the medical outcomes of illegal drug
use is the need to consider the consequences of the drugs themselves,
along with the consequences of their illegal status.

ETHNOGRAPHIC RESEARCH
IN RESPONSE TO THE HIV/AIDS EPIDEMIC

As the HIV/AIDS epidemic swept parts of the world in the 1980s
and 1990s, anthropologists who had studied injection drug use provided the details of needle sharing, one of the major modes of transmission of HIV. In a written genealogy of the use of ethnography to
study the details of drug use and its implications for HIV transmission, Nancy Campbell and Susan Shaw (2008) reached back to landmark qualitative studies of heroin addicts by Lindesmith and Dai in
1937, the work of Edward Preble and John Casey Jr. (1969) about life

on the streets as a heroin addict, and Michael Agar's classic *Ripping and Running: A Formal Ethnography of Urban Heroin Addicts* (1973). If ethnography could uncover the worldview of the injection drug user, then perhaps ethnography could unlock keys to HIV prevention.

An example of an ethnographic study of drug users is the multi-layered work of Page, Chitwood, Smith, Kane, and McBride (1990) among the intravenous drug users of Miami, Florida. Their goal was to study needle-using behaviors of out-of-treatment users. Among the methods of their study was observing needle-cleaning practices, syringe use, and accidental punctures, as well as conducting in-depth interviews to uncover what, if any, interventions could be used with this population to decrease the risk of HIV transmission. This study was one of the first to refute the folk wisdom of the time, which saw the behavior of drug addicts as nihilistic, as well as drug crazed and unreachable by rational approaches.

The Miami team observed behaviors that were risky in terms of HIV transmission. Among the behaviors observed were:

- Needles being cleaned in water and then left lying in a coffee can for others to use
- Users sometimes squirting the drugs from their own syringe directly into another person's syringe
- Two users drawing drugs from the same unheated bottle cap

To help eliminate risky behavior, the owners of "shooting galleries" or safe houses could potentially be recruited to learn about and enforce using clean needles, thereby eliminating or reducing behaviors that transmit the HIV virus.

After two decades of public health strategies of harm reduction by providing clean needles and condoms to prevent HIV, Campbell and Shaw (2008) reported instances in which ethnographers observed needle sharing, but the individuals being observed were still using the *discourse* of harm reduction. For example, the excerpt below is a summary of a direct observation of heroin drug use:

> When Juan was asked if his syringe was new, he responded, "Yes. It is second used." Susan asked, "Where did you get it?" and Juan answered, "I bought it on the [a nearby street]," then volunteered, "I didn't use it. A friend of mine did." (Campbell and Shaw 2008:703)

In addition to the public health discourse being at odds with direct observation, Campbell and Shaw also discuss the limitations of the philosophy of agencies that fund ethnographic research on HIV transmission. The funders are specifically interested in high-risk behaviors (injection drug use, unprotected sex) but are not necessarily interested in the larger social reality that drug users face, such as extreme poverty, that impinge on their health choices.

ETHNOGRAPHIC METHODS TO
MONITOR NEW DRUGS: THE CASE OF ILLY

Ethnographic research methods have been used as an effective tool in the discovery of new drugs or new drug combinations that portions of the population may be using. As ethnographers immersed themselves in drug-using communities in order to understand behaviors that could lead to HIV infection, they discovered that desperate drug users were exchanging sex for drugs and practicing high-risk behaviors (no condoms, multiple partners) even if the drugs themselves were not being used intravenously (Singer, Juvalis, Weeks, 2000). In a community study in Hartford, Connecticut, a team of researchers, following a group of out-of-treatment active drug users, found that some were smoking illy, which is marijuana soaked in embalming fluid. Users of illy reported a long-lasting high that involved hallucinations, no memory of the events that took place when high, physical confrontations with others, violence, and risky behavior such as walking into traffic. One of the study's community consultants said:

> I was over at a friend of mine house. . . . And he asked, me did I want to smoke. I said, yeah. And I sat there and rolled it. I didn't know what—it's reefer but—the reason why you call it that [i.e., illy] is because it make you ill . . . do some weird stupid stuff. . . . Make you think you can beat everybody, that you Superman. (Singer et al. 2000:378)

In Hartford, illy use was concentrated among younger and newer drug users who had not been using cocaine or heroin. The embalming fluid used to make illy contains formaldehyde, which is known to produce vomiting, coma, weakness, convulsions, kidney damage, and possibly death (Hawkins, Schwartz-Thompson, and Kahane 1994). Why would such a potentially lethal substance be added to marijuana (and in some cases, tobacco)? Singer and colleagues (2000) see the introduction of new drugs or "enhanced" drugs as a part of the wider consumer culture, where new products are constantly introduced and promoted to expand markets and profits.

The ethnographic team worked closely with the State Department of Public Health, with local health, drug treatment, and human service providers, and with criminal justice professionals to discuss the rising rate of illy use and its implication for drug use prevention, treatment, and HIV risk reduction. The researchers suggested that prevention efforts should include narratives of the negative experiences that current illy users have as a way to warn potential users.

CONCLUSION

As we have seen, drugs can be used to relieve pain, intensify experiences, induce euphoria, communicate with the supernatural, among many other uses. Drugs, both legal and illegal, as well as the drug trade and incarceration due to drugs, take a severe toll on human life.

Generally the use of indigenous drugs in a ritualized manner is contrasted with the desperation of the drug addict. However, we may ask ourselves if this dichotomy reflects reality and the full range of human experiences, or if it is an artifact of our need for discrete categories related to the value-laden topic of drug use. In thinking about the role of culture in the use of drugs, is there cultural knowledge we can use to help people recover from addiction? The next chapter will review some of the major approaches to recovery that can be utilized for people who are dependent on alcohol, tobacco, or drugs.

EXPERIENTIAL LEARNING ACTIVITIES

• As was the case in learning about alcohol cultures, interview an international student on campus about the diverse drug use cultures in his or her country. A difference between asking about drugs and alcohol is that the student may come from a country in which drugs are grown for export to the United States, Canada, or Europe, or where the country is one through which drugs pass on their way to the industrialized world. In the interview, you can ask about the differential enforcement of drug laws that may depend on the ethnicity, region, social class, or other culturally important factors.

• You may also interview an "elder" who has lived through various stages of drug use and drug penalties. For example, many of today's students have parents who lived during the 1960s and 1970s, when ideas about drug use may have been quite different than they are today. How does the person explain such differences?

The promotion of Alcoholics Anonymous in Poland.

Chapter Five

Recovery in Cross-Cultural Perspective

Everybody's got to walk that lonesome valley, they got to walk it by theirselves. There's nobody here can walk it for them, they've got to walk it by theirselves. ("Lonesome Valley" by A. P. Carter)

Although recovery from alcohol, tobacco, or drug addiction is an individual struggle as portrayed above, recovery, like use and misuse, is an expression of culture. In this chapter we examine a sampling of some of the most widely used models of recovery, such as the mutual help movement, as well as lesser known approaches to healing, such as the work of aboriginal Elders helping those within the confines of prisons. An important challenge within the field of recovery is to demonstrate, through scientifically acceptable means, that the method of recovery actually works (it is *efficacious*). Selectively remembering the successes or incorrectly attributing the success to the method of recovery and not to something else does not result in an accurate evaluation of a recovery method. Another challenge is to ask: If a recovery method is discovered, through research, to be efficacious, can it be exported beyond a research setting (is it *effective* when applied to real-world situations)?

There is a modest anthropological literature on treatment of and recovery from addictions, including ethnographies of therapeutic communities (e.g., Skoll 1992) and a linguistic analysis of the language of recovery and how both therapists and those in recovery learn the "script" that is so often used in putting the recovery process into

75

words (e.g., Carr 2011). However, the potential of anthropology's contribution to tailoring treatments and recovery to the needs of people trying to end their addictions has not been fully realized (Hunt and Barker 1999; Page and Singer 2010). In this chapter we look at the language of recovery, models of treatment, how to determine treatment efficacy, and Alcoholics Anonymous (AA) from a cross-cultural perspective. We will examine questions of when and why treatments diffuse, explore examples of utilizing indigenous treatments, look at example of how to make treatment and prevention culturally congruent, and discuss the value of using ethnographic methods as a way to improve treatment and recovery programs.

THE LANGUAGE OF RECOVERY

There are myriad words used to describe the process of extricating oneself from addictions to substances, and each one carries with it its own cultural and historical baggage. William White (2008, 2011) provides an excellent deconstruction of what words such as *treatment, recovery,* and *recovering* mean. Treatment suggests professionally directed intervention that is done with the addicted person. Recovery suggests a process through which people achieve an overall enhanced quality of life (SAMHSA 2009). The word recovery is most often associated with the mutual help movement, most prominently Alcoholics Anonymous (AA) and its many offspring (e.g., Narcotics Anonymous (NA). As the addictions treatment field grew in terms of numbers of professionals in the mid-20th century, recovery was often seen as an adjunct to treatment and a method of aftercare when treatment was over. Recently, the word "recovery" has become widespread outside of the mutual help movement, although it is not clear whether it is the word or the concept that is now being embraced (White 2011). In addition to the treatment/recovery duality is the issue of the use of the present participle form, *recovering*, denoting the action is in progress, as opposed to the past participle form, *recovered*, denoting the action is complete. The word "recovering" conveys the process of achieving an intended outcome (e.g., sobriety) but, as White (2011) argues, may not give proper recognition to those who have been free of their symptoms of addiction for many years. The term *healing* is often used for approaches that include a strong spiritual element, such as the healing that may come about for a Native American working with an Elder.

CURRENT MODELS OF RECOVERY/TREATMENT

Before turning to an anthropological view of specific methods of recovery, it is important to be aware of the current most widely utilized forms of help for addictions in the United States. The National Institute on Drug Abuse (2009) categorizes approaches to addictions treatment as behavioral treatments, medications, and residential treatment. Behavioral treatments include cognitive-behavioral therapy (using strategies to alter cognitions about a task or situation), multidimensional family therapy (designed for adolescents and their families), and motivational interviewing (a widely used treatment approach that supports the individual's desire to change according to his or her own values). Medications include methadone, buprenorphine, and naltrexone for the treatment of addiction to opiates; nicotine replacement therapies and bupropion for addiction to nicotine; and natrexone and acamprosate for treating alcohol dependence. Residential treatment includes therapeutic communities that are structured residences that utilize staff in recovery. In addition to these treatments, the National Institute on Alcohol Abuse and Alcoholism (NIAAA 2000) lists 12-step self-help programs (e.g., AA), motivational enhancement therapy, couples therapy, and brief interventions. The NIAAA is also testing the treatment of addiction to alcohol and nicotine together. For those people who have both substance abuse problems as well as serious mental illness (called co-occurring disorders), the approach called Assertive Community Treatment (ACT), which features a small caseload for each counselor, community outreach, and a multidisciplinary team approach (including nurses, psychiatrists, social workers), is being tested throughout the world (Burns 2010).

DEMONSTRATING EFFICACY IN HEALING

The "gold standard" of scientific research of treatment efficacy is the randomized double blind placebo-controlled trial, which is most often used to test new medications. Here people are randomly assigned to the experimental group (those people receive the drug being tested) or to the control condition (those people receive a *placebo*, which is an inert substance that looks and tastes like the drug under study). Neither the participants nor the treatment providers know which individuals are in which group, thus it is "double blinded". An example of the randomized double blind placebo-controlled trial is a study that tried to assess the efficacy of acamprosate, which had been shown to have some success in relapse prevention for alcohol-dependent people when combined with counseling and social support (Whitworth and Fischer 1996). In this study, 455 alcohol-dependent patients were randomly assigned to treatment with acamprosate or to a placebo, which was identical in appearance to the acamprosate tablets, for 360 days. At the end of this period, 18.3% of the acamprosate-treated patients had been continually abstinent compared to 7.1% of the placebo group. This was a statistically significant difference that indicated that acamprosate could be effective as an adjunct to psychosocial and behavioral treatment for a portion of alcohol-dependent individuals.

Daniel Moerman (2000), in analyzing the research about the effect of placebos in various world cultures, made an important discovery: those people who got a placebo instead of the drug under study varied widely in their reaction to the placebo. For example, in three studies from Brazil, the placebo healing rate for an antacid ulcer medication averaged 7% in contrast to 36% in the rest of the world. On the other hand, in six studies in Germany, the placebo healing rate for ulcer medications averaged 59%, almost twice as high as the rest of the world, and almost three times higher than in the average of 22% for the placebo effect in Denmark and the Netherlands (Moerman 2000).

When we turn to treatment studies that compare behavioral interventions as opposed to pharmacologic interventions, it is possible to conduct randomized controlled trials, albeit not double blinded ones. For example, in a study that compared the efficacy of multidimensional family therapy (MDFT) involving a peer group intervention with primarily low-income teens in the United States, Liddle and colleagues (2009) randomly assigned the adolescents to either the treatment condition (MDFT) or the control condition (peer group intervention). The 12-month follow-up indicated that MDFT resulted in a statistically significant reduction in substance use, delinquency, internalized distress, and problems within the adolescent's family, peer group, and school, in comparison to the peer group intervention. This study could not have been double blinded since the therapists for each condition, as well as the participants, were aware of the behavioral interventions.

When the interventions for addiction are professionally directed (such as motivational interviewing), efficacy is tested through randomized controlled trials. In contrast, many studies of nonprofessional healing have depended on descriptive studies that may or may not have included a comparison group, though not usually a randomized control group. An exception to this has been outcome research regarding Alcohol Anonymous (AA), a nonprofessional treatment for alcohol misuse, which has been studied extensively in the last 20 years.

ALCOHOLICS ANONYMOUS:
A CULTURALLY MALLEABLE RECOVERY MODEL

On any given day in the United States there are more than 700,000 people who receive alcoholism treatment (NIAAA 2000). AA is the most frequently utilized form of treatment (McKellar, Stewart, and Humphreys 2003), with an estimated one million members in the United States alone. AA began as, and is still, a home-grown method of help that in many ways is culturally congruent to the Protestant Middle America of its founders and has managed to be culturally malleable as it has traveled around the world. AA is the most frequently evaluated nonprofessional treatment model in the field of addictions.

The roots of AA began in the 1920s and 1930s with the rise of the Protestant evangelical movement called the Oxford Group (Humphreys 2004). The group valued confession of and restitution for one's sins. A member of an Oxford Group, Edwin Thatcher, as a part of his evangelism, reached out to his friend William Griffith Wilson, who later became Bill W., cofounder of AA, who was struggling to stop drinking. Subsequently, Bill W. had what he called a spiritual awakening while undergoing alcohol detoxification and was able to stop drinking. During a business trip to Akron in May 1935, when he felt tempted to drink again, he called up his friend, Dr. Robert Holbrook Smith (Dr. Bob) who was also struggling with alcoholism, and the two talked for several hours and gave each other the strength not to drink. Thus began AA.

By 1939 AA had broken with the Oxford Group and diffused quickly throughout the United States and eventually around the world. The central written texts for AA became known as the 12 Steps, a course of action for recovery, and the 12 Traditions, the guidelines and principles for the group and for a group's interrelationships among its members as well as among other 12-step groups (Alcoholics Anonymous World Services, Inc. 2008).

One can still see elements of the Oxford Group in AA's steps: its concern with spirituality, more broadly defined than the Christianity of the original (steps 1–3, 11), making a moral inventory (steps 4–7, 10), making amends for one's failings (steps 8–9), and carrying the message (evangelism) to other alcoholics (step 12) The mutual help model of AA has generated at least 13 additional 12-step organizations that are organized around a personal problem (Mäkelä et al. 1996) including Overeaters Anonymous, Gamblers Anonymous, and Debtors Anonymous.

The 12 Steps of Alcoholics Anonymous

1. We admitted we were powerless over alcohol, and that our lives had become unmanageable.
2. Came to believe that a Power greater than ourselves could restore us to sanity.
3. Made a decision to turn our will and our lives over to the care of God *as we understood Him.*
4. Made a searching and fearless moral inventory of ourselves.
5. Admitted to God, to ourselves, and to another human being the exact nature of our wrongs.
6. Were entirely ready to have God remove all these defects of character.
7. Humbly asked Him to remove our shortcomings.
8. Made a list of all persons we had harmed, and became willing to make amends to them all.
9. Made direct amends to such people wherever possible, except when to do so would injure them or others.
10. Continued to take personal inventory and when we were wrong promptly admitted it.
11. Sought through prayer and meditation to improve our conscious contact with God *as we understood Him,* praying only for knowledge of His will for us and the power to carry that out.
12. Having had a spiritual awakening as the result of these steps, we tried to carry this message to alcoholics, and to practice these principles in all our affairs.

(A. A. World Services, Inc. 2008)

The 12 Traditions of Alcoholics Anonymous

1. Our common welfare should come first; personal recovery depends upon A.A. unity.
2. For our group purpose there is but one ultimate authority—a loving God as He may express Himself in our group conscience. Our leaders are but trusted servants; they do not govern.
3. The only requirement for A.A. membership is a desire to stop drinking.
4. Each group should be autonomous except in matters affecting other groups or A.A. as a whole.
5. Each group has but one primary purpose—to carry its message to the alcoholic who still suffers.
6. An A.A. group ought never endorse, finance, or lend the A.A. name to any related facility or outside enterprise, lest problems of money, property, and prestige divert us from our primary purpose.
7. Every A.A. group ought to be fully self-supporting, declining outside contributions.

8. Alcoholics Anonymous should remain forever nonprofessional, but our service centers may employ special workers.

9. A.A., as such, ought never be organized; but we may create service boards or committees directly responsible to those they serve.

10. Alcoholics Anonymous has no opinion on outside issues; hence the A.A. name ought never be drawn into public controversy.

11. Our public relations policy is based on attraction rather than promotion; we need always maintain personal anonymity at the level of press, radio, and films.

12. Anonymity is the spiritual foundation of all our Traditions, ever reminding us to place principles before personalities.

(A.A. World Services, Inc.)

The four essential characteristics of mutual help organizations are: (1) the members share a problem or condition; (2) there are no fees; (3) members participate on a voluntary basis; and (4) the goals involve personal change. The groups are characterized by reciprocal relationships of giving and receiving help (Humphreys 2004).

AA now exists in 60 countries throughout the world. In its diffusion, AA is flexible in adapting to the cultures where is exists. For example, in a two-year ethnography of an AA meeting in Mexico City, Brandes (2002) found that the 12th tradition of AA, anonymity, is not culturally congruent, at least in the working-class Mexico City meetings he attended. Here, the members lived and worked together and some were family. In addition to not maintaining anonymity, people could come in and out of the meeting freely, and at times meetings were held in only semi-enclosed places. The essence of the helping in this AA meeting, according to Brandes, came from the personal stories (called *historials* in Spanish) that people told each other. Newcomers, who were clearly not used to public speaking, found it hard to talk for several minutes in front of others. Once people had been attending for several months, they often could present their alcohol problem/recovery narratives for a full 15 minutes. The fact that the group accepted Brandes—a North American professor who told the group that he wanted to learn about AA and write a book about the meetings—into their ranks for two years is a reflection of their flexibility.

According to Brandes, the long tradition of *compadrazgo* (coparenting) in the Spanish-speaking world makes it possible for people to adapt to the AA sponsorship tradition. The *compadre* (or *comadre* in the case of women) relationship is the one that exists between the parents of the child and the child's godparents. It is a kind of "coparenting" that does not have its own term in English. Compadre/comadre now indicates a very close relationship that is generalized beyond the parent–godparent religious obligations of Catholicism. Brandes notes that most people came to the meetings he attended with a sponsor who gave the person moral support and encouragement.

There are countries where AA has spread that are not necessarily culturally congruent with some of its main tenets. In an excellent review of the diffusion of AA in eight countries other than the United States, Mäkelä and colleagues (1996) demonstrate AA's malleability as it became more culturally congruent within each country.

For example, steps 2 and 3 refer to a "Power greater than ourselves" and to "God," originally referring to a Christian concept of God. Mäkelä and colleagues found a range of belief in God, from 13% in Sweden to 56% in Poland. Some people identify the concept of a "higher power," to mean the AA fellowship itself. Some examples from the life stories of Finnish AA members include:

> "I consider the AA community and the program to be a Higher Power in the sense that they are clearly smarter things than what I myself could have ever been able to create." (Mäkelä et al. 1996:160)

> "I look at myself as a humanist. My Higher Power is inside me, something that exists inside human beings." (Mäkelä et al. 1996:160)

Steps 8 and 9, which refer to making amends for past wrongs, also may not be culturally congruent in some contexts. Again, an example from Finland indicates the inappropriateness of making amends verbally:

> "As separate performances, Steps Eight and Nine are alien to Finnish culture. We do not thresh human relationships, and we do not ask for or give absolution in so many words. I cannot bulldoze my parents into an emotional discussion. Change is not expressed in words but in behavior." (Mäkelä et al. 1996:156)

Another example of what many in the United States think is AA de rigueur is what Mäkelä and colleagues refer to as "positive politeness," which is giving positive feedback and support to others (e.g., "thank you Bob for sharing your story with us"). This is in contrast to "negative politeness," which Mäkelä defines as honoring an individual's autonomy rather than his or her need for approval. Finland and Iceland represent negative politeness cultures, where AA rituals such as holding hands at the end of the meetings or having everyone say in unison, "Hi Bob," after an introduction, is considered "intruding, embarrassing, and ridiculous" (Mäkelä et al. 1996:149). Here, too, AA has shown itself to be adaptable to different cultures while at the same time retaining its mutual help aspect.

The two final examples of the cultural malleability of AA are groups that separated from the organization in order to express their cultural orientation. The groups are Women for Sobriety (WFS) and Jewish Alcoholics, Chemically Dependent Persons, and Significant Others (JACS).

Jean Kilpatrick, a sociologist, formed WFS in 1973 in order to counter the male emphasis she experienced in AA (Humphreys 2004). A major focus of WFS is on building up a woman's self-esteem, rather than countering the grandiosity of men (as in AA). WFS does not utilize sponsors or encourage lifelong membership to counter undue dependency, even on AA. There is also no reference to a higher power. Intellectual analysis of one's problems is encouraged. Instead of using the AA introduction, "Hi, I'm Jean and I'm an alcoholic," the WFS introduction is, "I am Jean and I am a competent woman."

JACS was formed in 1979 by Jewish AA members who felt uncomfortable with the Christian overtones (e.g., ending meetings with a Christian prayer) of some AA meetings (Humphreys 2004). They also wanted to be able to freely discuss some special aspects of being alcohol-dependent and Jewish, since alcoholism in the past has been considered a Gentile problem by Jews and is highly stigmatized. The JACS website, http://www.jacsweb.org, provides links to meetings and activities in the United States and some international activity. There are also some culturally meaningful announcements, such as ones that invite members to "celebrate a clean and sober Seder or Purim," referring to two Jewish holidays in which drinking wine is a part of the observance. One can celebrate these holidays, but substitute a nonalcoholic beverage for wine.

Efficacy of Alcoholics Anonymous

There are some inherent difficulties in ascertaining the efficacy of AA, since it is a self-help, voluntary, anonymous organization, with no records kept and little hierarchy. In recent decades, however, AA has been studied in order to evaluate its efficacy in decreasing alcohol dependence. Most studies of AA have attempted to *correlate* AA attendance and abstinence from drinking. Correlational studies generally indicate an association between a treatment method and an outcome, but do not indicate the fact that the treatment necessarily *caused* the outcome.

The correlational studies found that greater AA participation was associated with less drinking and fewer alcohol-related problems, such as drunk driving (McKellar et al. 2003). In order to examine whether this is due to an initially greater depth of motivation, researchers tracked 2,319 alcohol-dependent male veterans for one to two years after their treatment at one of 15 inpatient programs of the VA in order to discover whether or not AA involvement was correlated with better outcomes of less severe drinking (McKellar et al. 2003). Given the same levels of severity of alcohol problems, the same prior AA experience, and the same level of motivation before treatment, those who attended AA after the VA treatment more regularly had greater positive outcomes. The authors hypothesize that AA involvement appeared to *nurture* motivation to change alcohol use within the person, so that even those without great initial motivation to change benefitted from AA involvement and attendance.

There have been randomized controlled trials wherein alcohol-dependent individuals are referred to AA or to another standard alcohol treatment (such as motivational enhancement or cognitive behavioral therapy) and followed to discover the impact of AA on them. A variant of this type of study is to use Twelve Step Facilitation, in which the clinician works with the patient to encourage him or her to attend a 12-step meeting such as AA (Humphreys 1999). In a randomized study, the AA group and the non-AA group will be the same for pretreatment characteristics such as years of drinking and severity of alcohol dependence. Lee Ann Kaskutas (2009), in an excellent overview of AA effectiveness research, reports that in the rigorous randomized studies, two showed AA effectiveness, one did not find statistically significant differences between the AA condition and the control condition, and one found that the people randomized to AA fared worse. In some of the studies, however, the researchers were not sure that people who were assigned to the *non*-AA treatment group did not in fact go to AA anyway, which would cloud the comparisons.

Many AA members stress that AA is a spiritual program, which is reinforced by its 12 steps. Since spirituality as a concept is difficult to define or operationalize in efficacy research, often this important aspect of AA is either ignored or is interpreted in the psychological language of social support. Maria Gabrielle Swora (2004) deconstructs the 12 steps of AA using the concepts of sacred healing, which involve a higher power and a person's spirit or inner-nature, that have been applied worldwide to religious healing. Swora sees an internal logic within the 12 steps that explicates AA's focus on fellowship, the program itself, and spirituality.

In the transformative rhetoric of healing, the individual sufferer needs to be convinced that healing is necessary and possible, as presented in steps 1 and 2. The individual then surrenders to an other-than-human power, as in step 3. Swora observes an AA member embracing this third step, after struggling to do so:

> He decided to think of God as the good manifested in everything and everybody, but particularly people in AA. When he saw the good in others, he suddenly recognized the good in himself, and he wept. He described this experience as profoundly spiritual and claimed that it marked the beginning of his sobriety for him. (Swora 2004:195)

Steps 4 and 5 comprise the moral inventory, which is seen as a life review and a kind of confession. These steps often manifest shame and fear, but now the individual likely has the support of a trusted AA sponsor. As Swora heard in one of the AA meetings she attended:

> A young woman who had typed out her Fourth Step on her computer like a term paper described feeling utterly dismayed when her sponsor refused to look at her work and instead said, "Start reading." (Swora 2004:197)

AA members describe their sense of relief and freedom after taking their fourth and fifth steps. These steps are sometimes taken many times in the course of recovery.

Steps 6 and 7 ask the person to be continually open to change. Here the alcoholic is ready to look at his or her entire life and shortcomings, whether they directly relate to alcohol or not, and confront the challenges of change.

Steps 8 and 9 involve making amends to persons whom the individual may have hurt and to repair the damage, if it is possible. Here the emphasis, as is the case in traditional healing systems, is on the person and his or her relationship to his or her social world.

The final three steps involve keeping up the AA program of recovery. Especially in step 12, the individual is encouraged to work with other people in recovery by, for example, visiting people in treatment facilities. Often people talk about increasing their 12th-step work when they themselves are feeling shaky in their sobriety (Swora 2004).

WHEN DOES A TREATMENT NOT DIFFUSE?

When does a treatment that one would think would be adopted not diffuse? This is an appropriate question for anthropologists to confront because culture and context are important components to finding the answer. Understanding the cultural context into which treatment has been introduced can lead to knowing why it did or did not diffuse. In the classic work on the diffusion of innovation, Rogers (1995) suggested there are many good ideas that never become practice. Generally, innovations that become adopted have a relative advantage over alternatives and are compatible with the existing culture. A classic example of the lack of diffusion of an idea is the failure of a two-year campaign to promote water boiling in a Peruvian village to prevent the spread of waterborne infectious diseases such as typhoid. After two years, the full-time village health worker had convinced only five out of 200 housewives to boil their drinking water. In an analysis of what went wrong, Wellin (1955) suggested the water-boiling campaign violated strong cultural beliefs (only sick people drink boiled water), the village health worker was herself an outsider to the village, and the housewives were not village opinion makers but were marginalized members of the community.

Two interesting cases of the lack of diffusion are the slow growth of AA in Russia and the slow growth of Nicotine Anonymous, the

12-step program for nicotine dependence, in the United States. In both cases, one might think a low-cost accessible source of help for addictions would be welcome.

Drinking has long been a fact of life in Russia. From the 1540s, when Ivan IV began to establish taverns in all of the major towns, with revenues from sales going directly to the royal treasury, through the Soviet and post-Soviet period, the sale of vodka has been vital to the Russian economy (Herlihy 2002). The population of Russia is less than half of the population of the United States, yet it is estimated that Russia is the largest consumer of spirits (hard liquor) in the world, with the 1999 estimate of 6.5 liters per person per year. In contrast, the United States ranked 19th in the world, with an estimated 1.9 liters per person per year (*World Drink Trends*, 2000). It is estimated that over half of male deaths in three Russian cities during the years 1990–2001 were related to alcohol consumption ("Alcohol and Harm Reduction in Russia" 2009). Russian men have a life expectancy of 59 years in contrast to 75.3 years in the US (CDC Press Release 2009). It is estimated that 40,000 men die of alcohol poisoning each year in Russia, often from drinking alcohol products not meant for consumption, such as cologne.

In 2001, while I was on a trip to Russia with the National Institute on Alcohol Abuse and Alcoholism to test a new social work curriculum, a group of AA members in St. Petersburg asked me, as an anthropologist, to try to uncover some of the reasons for the slow diffusion of AA (Glasser 2002). At the time, there were 20 active meetings in St. Petersburg. By 2005 there were reported to be 300 meetings in all of Russia (*The Moscow Times* July 15, 2005). Contrast such figures with the 55,244 AA groups currently in the United States (http://www.aa.org).

Given the depth of alcohol problems in Russia, why has AA not diffused? Critchlow (2001) hypothesized that two explanations for the slow growth of AA in Russia may have been the lack of referrals to AA by physicians who may believe that they will be replaced by AA, thereby reducing their income, and the belief by some Russian Orthodox clergymen that AA is a foreign religious cult. Kagan and Shafer (2001) suggested that during the early period of AA in Russia, people avoided the AA meetings because of their resemblance to "collective ideologies." Moreover, people resisted the concept of a higher power. AA materials were expensive to print, so the organization was not able to use printed matter to promote itself and its meetings, and it was difficult for individuals to find out about meetings. Egorova (2002) suggested additional possible reasons: insufficient mass media coverage of AA; a perception that AA is a Western and ideologically alien movement; a lack of observance of traditions of anonymity in Russia; an absence of "beacons" who are AA members with long-term sobriety and AA membership; and the fact that AA groups move frequently, change their meeting times, and in general aren't always accessible to interested persons. Further investigation is needed to discover the paradox of why a nation that appears to be in need of affordable approaches for alcoholism has not embraced AA as one of its approaches (Glasser 2003).

Cigarette use is the leading preventable cause of death in the United States among adults (see chapter 3). Yet, the 12-step program designed for smoking cessation, Nicotine Anonymous (NicA), has not diffused widely, nor has it received attention from providers of health care or from the research community. NicA began in California in 1985 by AA members who wanted to work on their nicotine addiction using the 12-step approach. Although there has been a decline in cigarette use in the United States from approximately 42% in 1965 to 20.5% in 2004, there is evidence that nicotine dependence among cigarette smokers may actually have increased, especially among women cigarette users living in poverty (Goodwin, Keyes, and Hasin 2009). Further, there is recent evidence that some heavy smokers are interested in approaches to cessation that include a spiritual dimension (Gonzales et al. 2007). The accessibility of smoking cessation programs, in contrast to recovery programs to quit using alcohol or drugs, is often minimal, is not offered consistently, and is not free. In my own research with homeless populations, I see almost no evidence of individuals being offered help to quit smoking.

In 1999 there were reported to be 450 NicA groups (Lichtenstein 1999), and in 2010 there were approximately 328 in the United States according to the NicA website (https://www.nicotine-anonymous.org). This lack of diffusion of NicA is puzzling, and we can only offer some hypotheses in need of testing. One is that NicA came about during an era where there was a demand for *evidence-based* interventions. NicA has not been the subject of treatment efficacy research and is therefore not included as an evidence-based treatment. Like AA, NicA functions outside of the world of health professionals, and its advocates tend to be former smokers who believe they were helped by the program. The fact that so few groups exist means that people who might want to participate can't because they don't live close to a location where a group meets. Using NicA as a constant source of support, as people do with AA, is difficult (Glasser 2010).

UTILIZING INDIGENOUS CULTURE IN RECOVERY

I used to love drugs. I used to love drinking. Now I love going to the sweats. I replaced that addiction. I have become addicted to spirituality.

—Aboriginal inmate interviewed by James Waldram (1997:129)

Indigenous healing involves methods of recovery that have not generally been the subject of efficacy studies. These indigenous approaches are often geared to restoring harmony within the afflicted individual as well as between the person, their physical environments, and the spirit world. Indigenous practices, approaches, and beliefs may incorporate plants, animals, and natural resources; spiritual therapies; and physical techniques to diagnose, treat, and prevent illness or maintain good health.

An example of indigenous healing is the utilization of aboriginal spirituality as a form of symbolic healing. The term *aboriginal* is used throughout Canada to refer to First Nations, Inuit, and Métis people. Working in Canadian prisons, James Waldram (1997) carefully documented the various healing rituals used behind the prison walls among aboriginal prisoners who suffered from alcohol and drug abuse as well as the effects of child abuse and violence. The aboriginal healing practice used in the prison might involve participating in sweat lodges (a hut in which water is poured over hot coals to produce steam that is a part of the ritual purification in healing), talking with an Elder, forming a drumming circle (communal drumming of Native songs; in some communities, people must come to the drumming circle sober and drug free), passing around a sacred pipe, or burning tobacco and sweetgrass. The aboriginal spiritual leader was not necessarily from the Native group of the prisoner and the prisoner was not necessarily fluent in the language the leader used when reciting prayers (e.g., Cree), yet prison personnel often remarked on the calm and tranquility that appears to overcome the person once involved in Native healing. An intriguing aspect to this work is that many of the aboriginal prisoners had no experience with Native culture before entering prison. A lingering question is how feasible is it for the prisoners to continue to pursue Native healing once they leave the prison?

Aboriginal healing is often facilitated by an Elder who is a teacher of a specific Native tradition as well as a guide to the individual. An example is Salteaux Elder Papaquash, who allowed Waldram to observe his healing sessions with Canadian prisoners. The text below provides an explanation by Papaquash of the personal sorrows experienced by the prisoners and a pathway out of the misery that is based on a communal understanding of the wrongs done to aboriginal communities:

> Our ancestors warned and predicted that for many generations the people would have a hard time. A dark black cloud would surround and plague all of the peoples of the Earth. They foretold this dark black cloud would bring darkness into people's lives. They foretold that for many generations this dark black cloud would cause great sorrow and suffering. That many would become sick at heart. . . .
> It was foretold that the day would come when this dark cloud would weaken slowly at first and then diminish; and that the peo-

ple would reawaken slowly as if from a long drugged sleep. It was also said that these things would come to pass, and that the seventh generation would rise and become strong. They would do this by seeking out the ancient teachings of our forefathers. (Waldram 1997:82)

One of the prisoners interviewed by Waldram was preparing to participate in the Sun Dance when he returned to the community as a way to fulfill a vow to help heal his sick son. The Sun Dance is a good example of a rite of intensification, which can reaffirm a person's commitment to his community. In one variation of the Sun Dance, the participant (always a male) has the muscles in his chest and upper back pierced. A skewer is then attached to a thong that is attached to a rope, which has been attached to a pole. The dancer then swings around the pole in order to free himself. Grobsmith says that for many young people the Sun Dance is a way to recover from alcoholism and gain strength and pride in their Indian culture (Grobsmith 1981).

A question that occurs when discussing any kind of culturally specific recovery method is whether the treatment can be exported to people in search of help who are not from the culture. An example of a treatment, which has been successfully exported from China and is widely practiced in the United States, is acupuncture. Another lesser known example is a Cree treatment for psoriasis. In a small pilot study in Edmonton, Alberta, Canada, a group of non-Native people with intractable psoriasis worked with a Cree Elder. Using salves made from trees, chanting, and sitting in a sweat lodge, most got some relief from their psoriasis (Young, Ingram, and Swartz 1989). Much more dubious is the commercial appropriation of Native healing. For example, three people died in a New Age style "vision quest" and sweat lodge ceremony in Arizona in 2009 after being directed to fast and then endure three hours of intense heat in a sweat lodge constructed of blankets and plastic and heated with fiery rocks (Dougherty 2009).

There are indications from pilot research that a meditation approach to addictions treatment from China, called *Qingong* (pronounced Chi Kung), may be effective when used in adult residential treatment programs for alcohol and drug addiction to reduce craving, anxiety, and withdrawal symptoms (Chen et al. 2010). In a US study with patients who were not familiar with Qingong, those patients who selected Qingong experienced better results than the group that selected the Stress Management and Relaxation Training (SMART), a standardized relaxation program that can be used to reduce craving, anxiety, and withdrawal symptoms. More rigorous testing of Qingong is needed before it can be called an efficacious adjunct to treatment.

INCREASING THE CULTURAL CONGRUENCE
OF TREATMENTS AND PREVENTION

Christine Daley and her team (2006) sought to discover how to modify the Second Wind smoking cessation curriculum that was developed by the Muscogee Nation of Oklahoma's Tobacco Prevention Program for use in a pan-Indian setting, where members of many nations would participate. The goal was to make the curriculum even more culturally appropriate for Native Americans. The curriculum was based on the American Cancer Society's FreshStart program, which is four face-to-face group support sessions (http://www.acsworkplacesolutions.com/freshstart.asp) led by a trained facilitator. FreshStart includes: motivational intervention activities, counseling, social support, and education about medication and approaches to quitting.

The Daley team conducted six focus groups with members of over 200 nations of Native Americans. The focus group participants said they wanted a more Native orientation for all of the printed material, including more Native images, colors, emphasis on oral history, and visual understanding. As one participant remarked about the current brochure: "I don't think this way. I don't do graphs. I don't do charts. I'm a Native person" (Daley et al. 2006:430).

In terms of content of the cessation program, the focus group participants suggested more discussion of traditional tobacco use and the sacredness of tobacco. They wanted the curriculum to acknowledge the difference between traditional tobacco use and recreational use, and they wanted an Elder to be the presenter about traditional use. The participants also wanted the facilitators of the program to be Native, and they wanted the sessions to be frequent at the beginning of their quit attempts.

The above recommendations have been incorporated into a new pan-Indian smoking cessation developed by the University of Kansas Medical Center. It is anticipated that if this pilot program is successful, it will eventually be the subject of rigorous efficacy testing.

Tobacco control professionals in both the US Indian Health Service (Grim 2007) and Health Canada's First Nations, Inuit and Aboriginal Health (http://www.hc-sc.gc.ca), recognize that any tobacco control and smoking cessation with Native communities should recognize and respect the thousands of years of history of the use of tobacco in ceremonies, rituals, prayers, and healing. There is a distinction made between the sacred use of tobacco and its recreational or secular use.

Since the knowledge of culture can promote tobacco use, can culture also be used to promote prevention or cessation of tobacco use? In 2006–2007 I was involved in two community billboard campaigns run by the Community Renewal Team, a large community action agency serving the poor communities in Hartford, Connecticut, and the surrounding region, in which members of the community of Hartford created the words and the images for the prevention and cessation billboards. The first campaign began with a poster contest for youth who were involved in an after-school program led by a smoking cessation health educator who helped the youth design images and messages for the billboards. A tobacco use prevention grant from the Connecticut Department of Health paid for the billboard space. When the winning posters became billboards and were hung on the sides of buildings throughout the predominantly poor neighborhoods of Hartford so that pedestrians could easily view them, the mayor held a press conference commending all of the youth participants, reinforcing their smoking prevention work.

The second campaign featured billboard images of adults from the community as they contemplated their reasons for quitting smoking. The images reflect the majority of the population in Hartford in terms of age and ethnicity, while the statements are the most frequently heard reasons for quitting.

We were not able to formally evaluate the effectiveness of these campaigns, but we designed them using a manual on "counter-marketing" campaigns published by the Centers for Disease Control (CDC 2010a). The grassroots counter-marketing billboard campaigns directly addressed the aggressive efforts of the tobacco industry's attempts to reach poor communities.

CHANGING THE CONTEXT OF RECOVERY

There is excellent literature on the cultural barriers to substance abuse treatment. For example, Shulamith Straussner Ashenberg (2001) presents scholarly work on issues related to 19 different ethnic groups in the United States who have substance abuse problems in need of treatment. Almost all of the authors of the articles are academics who have clinical experience in treatment of substance abuse and are themselves members of the groups under consideration. Often the group's history, worldview, experiences with mutual aid, religion, and the cultural context of life, which may include poverty, violence, and discrimination, are considered to help clinicians achieve what Straussner Ashenberg calls "ethnocultural competence" (Straussner Ashenberg 2001:7).

Culturally sensitive treatment is concerned not only with the worldviews of cultures and subcultures of the people seeking treatment but also with the context in which people live. In our research with homeless populations in Hartford, Connecticut, and Providence, Rhode Island, William Zywiak and I (Glasser and Zywiak 2003) found that 43% of Hartford's homeless population attributed their homelessness to drug and/or alcohol use, and 45% of the sample of Providence's homeless population had a lifetime history of alcohol abuse and still drank in the year preceding the interview. Despite this level of substance abuse, we found few examples of substance abuse treatment offered inside the shelters in either city. A key to substance abuse treatment in homeless populations is *outreach*—that is, offering treatment within the settings where people spend their time frequently and consistently, such as in soup kitchens and shelters. There is a literature on nonthreatening outreach and engagement for homeless people that has been tested in a variety of homeless settings, including public parks (Glasser and Bridgman 1999), which finds having the same outreach worker make contact with the person, for short visits at regular intervals, and bringing food or blankets (or other necessities), often is successful.

It is also important to test and modify current treatments in order to adapt them to homeless settings. However, in many efficacy studies, homelessness is an exclusion criterion for participation in the study. For example, Project MATCH was an eight-year, multi-million-dollar study that asked which types of alcohol-dependent individuals respond best to certain types of treatment. The study was a major test of some of the most promising substance abuse interventions (cognitive behavioral therapy, motivational enhancement, and 12-step facilitation). The study concluded that the three techniques are equal in effectiveness (Project MATCH Research Group 1993). Homeless populations were explicitly excluded from Project MATCH's study (Zerger 2002). Homeless individuals are often excluded from treatment studies because of the difficulty of finding the individuals for follow-up interviews. In reality, homeless individuals often stay close to their support services and networks.

Substance abuse treatment geared to homeless populations would have to pay attention to the daily survival needs that concern homeless individuals, including housing, food, clothing, and medical care. A promising approach to combining housing stability with treatment for both substance abuse and mental illness is called Housing First (Padgett, Gulcur, and Tsemberis 2006). Here, permanent housing that does not *require* treatment or abstinence as a prerequisite for living there is offered to people who are homeless and who have both mental illness and substance abuse symptoms. The premise is that, by first living in his or her own apartment, the person's life will become more stable. Once that happens, the individual can access treatment for his or her mental illness and substance abuse as well as take part in the vigorous support services that focus on recovery and community integration. In the meantime, homelessness is decreased within the community.

ETHNOGRAPHIC METHODS IN DRUG TREATMENT OUTCOME STUDIES

The inclusion of anthropologists on treatment outcome teams can lead to a better understanding of why some programs work and some don't. Ethnographic research methods (e.g., participant observation, open-ended interviews, focus groups) can elicit valuable data for evaluating current programs and approaches, which includes discovering which approaches are in need of change and determining the viability of new treatment techniques. The ethnographer, trained to enter a community *without* preconceived ideas and biases, attends to the insider's point of view. This training facilitates communication between the researcher and the study population. Ethnographers can also learn what the barriers are to treatment that may be unknown to professionals. They can learn why some treatments, which appear to hold promise during efficacy testing, do not appear to work as well when they are diffused into the treatment community outside of a research framework.

A good example of ethnographic methods' potential is the evaluation of three types of treatment delivery for substance-abusing homeless men. Men living in a large shelter who had a current substance abuse of alcohol and/or drugs were randomly assigned to three groups: a six-month comprehensive residential treatment group; a four- to nine-month shelter-based intensive case-management program; and the regular shelter's services provided by case managers with very large caseloads (Stahler et al. 1995). The researchers hypothesized that residential treatment would be more effective than shelter-based intensive case management, which would be more effective than clients using the usual shelter services. Yet, in follow-up assessments at six months after discharge, the researchers discovered very little difference in effectiveness among the three groups in terms of substance use, housing stability, employment, and psychological status.

During the study, the field researchers discovered that the clients in all three groups were able to utilize AA and NA meetings on a daily basis. Further, when the ethnographers interviewed the successful clients in all three groups, the clients said they attributed their success to the 12-step programs they attended (Stahler and Cohen 2000). Whereas the researchers were focused on the different residential situations as a basis for determining the most effective model for treatment delivery, it was help within the larger context of the homeless men's lives that contributed to positive results.

CONCLUSION

Considering recovery from alcohol, tobacco, and drugs through an anthropological lens involves looking at not only the *content* of the treatment but also at its *context*, that is, who had input in designing the treatment, how the recovery can be modified to fit the culture, and what the treatment means to the community. *Evidence-based* studies often involve determining a treatment's efficacy when it is tested in *ideal situations*. The decision about which treatments are subject to scientific inquiry is itself culturally determined. Furthermore, after an evidence-based treatment is introduced in communities, there is often a gap between its efficacy (the power to produce the intended effect) and its effectiveness in the community. Conducting ethnographic studies of substance abuse treatment as it is experienced in the context of daily life could unearth the puzzle over why, despite the success of treatments in experimental conditions, the treatments do not often translate into success "on the ground."

EXPERIENTIAL LEARNING ACTIVITIES

- **Attending a 12-Step Meeting:** Each student in the class will attend a meeting of one of the 12-step groups, such as Alcoholics Anonymous, Narcotics Anonymous, Cocaine Anonymous, or Nicotine Anonymous. Go on the group's website to find "open" meetings. You may want to attend a meeting outside your home community to avoid encountering someone you know. There is a protocol for visitors that you should follow (such as not contributing your ideas at the meeting so that members can share their stories). Write down your observations (field notes) *after* the meeting. Remember to use pseudonyms to maintain anonymity. Later, analyze your field notes for prominent themes.

  When discussing your visit with other students, talk about how the meetings varied by gender, social class, ethnicity, and any other factors that may have emerged. One question to explore is whether the meeting was responsive to varying subcultures. For example, some women's meetings do not emphasize being "powerless" on the grounds that many women are trying to become empowered and need to focus on ways to achieve that goal. Discuss the types of social activities outside the meeting that were being promoted as a way to live a sober life. For example, some AA groups sponsor all-day nondrinking gatherings during holidays such as Thanksgiving. How do 12-step meetings mirror some of the cultural responses to sobriety that other cultures have tried?

  Many students have told me that it takes all of the courage they have to walk into the 12-step meeting (mostly AA meetings). Once there, they are very impressed by the general openness of the members and how many people come to meetings who have been sober for many years. A typical statement from a student is:

  > I came out of the meeting feeling like a new person. I was exposed to a new way of living, of kindness and support that I have never experienced before.

  One student had been telling our class all semester about one of his friends who had gotten into so much trouble with alcohol he has to abstain and attend AA meetings with people a lot older than himself. Over spring break, my student decided to attend an AA meeting with his friend. They were both concerned about a third friend whose drinking was also out of control. At the meeting, the AA members made suggestions about how to find meetings and support the person's decision to quit. The student went on to say:

  > The meeting came to a close and they talked about next week's meeting and how they want to organize some barbeques and picnics with all the nice weather coming up. Many members got another cup of coffee and conversed with other members and socialized for some time. My friend and I talked with some mem-

bers and they said how nice it was for us to try and look out for our friend. They told me how nice it was to see me help and support my friends through this tough time in their lives. I felt the chills on my arms and realized how much of an impact I have on the lives of my friends.

- **Writing a Recovery Narrative:** Interview someone who has recovered from dependence on alcohol, tobacco, or drugs, keeping all names and places confidential. After you write the person's recovery narrative, ask yourself what the salient features of recovery were for him or her. For example, some people are greatly helped by gaining a new set of friends through a 12-step program and care less about the words and texts of recovery. Other people may talk about losing something very important to them as a last straw, thereby pushing them toward recovery. A person's addiction and recovery narrative may itself change over time and may be different with different audiences.

    One student arranged a Skype call with an old high school friend who was addicted to heroin and had been in and out of rehabilitation programs. The assignment was a good reason to try to reconnect, although not without some trepidation.

    > Seeing Tom for the first time in a while was very strange, but from what I can see he looked better, he didn't look sick anymore. I had a feeling things were going well. The first question I asked Tom was, are you better now? He said yes, but that's not the first time I had heard that.

    > Tom told me to look at something as he rolled up his sleeve and put his arm in front of the camera. I was stunned by what I saw. Because of the damage he caused his arm from his injection drug use, he was able to pull a flap of skin up off his arm. I wasn't really sure how to react, so I joked about it and told him I almost puked from looking at it. He laughed, something I haven't seen from him a while.

    Some students realize how challenging everyday life can be for a person recovering from addictions. One student wrote:

    > Bob says that the only time he still has a craving for a drink is when he smells it. On Thursday nights the busses are filled with students who have been drinking. He says that when he smells it, he wants it badly.

    As we can see, both attending a 12-step meeting and writing a recovery narrative are powerful ways to understand addiction. It tends to be a humbling experience that makes one question previously held beliefs regarding recovery from addiction.

Chapter Six

Concluding Thoughts

In these pages we have examined two of the major threads of anthropological inquiry regarding addiction and recovery. The first thread is the insights gained from the great trove of ethnographic research that seeks to learn about a culture from the inside. From Bunzel's and Heath's detailed descriptions of ritualized drinking among indigenous people in Latin America to the finely tuned portrayals of injection drug users in a Los Angeles encampment by Bourgois and Schonberg, we are able to enter the culture of substance use and misuse as it is lived.

The second thread is anthropology's ability to step back and examine broad contexts in which people operate. We have asked the questions, for example, how does the language of addiction and recovery color our views? How do classification systems, such as drug scheduling or diagnostic categories, have implications for action? Why do some types of treatment or recovery find favor and become widespread, while others do not? What is the human cost of our elaborate system of drug prohibition?

The chapter on alcohol presented examples of how individuals and cultures learn to drink and how they learn to act when intoxicated. Ethnographic studies were the first to challenge the belief that alcohol has the same effects on all people. The consequences of drinking, including drinking to intoxication, cover the gamut, from benign and community building to dangerous and lethal for individuals and communities. The ethnographies that included detailed descriptions of drinking in many ways created the field of "the anthropology of addictions."

The tobacco chapter explored the fascinating case of a widely diffused mind-altering plant (when ingested) that was quickly adopted by Europeans who first encountered it in the New World. The physiological dependence that nicotine creates, along with tobacco's great economic profitability, means the tobacco industry has had much incentive to continually expand the pool of smokers. Further, governments have benefited historically from the significant amount of taxes derived from tobacco sales. In the current era of decreased rates of smoking in the industrialized world, there is a great incentive for tobacco companies to uncover new markets, often using knowledge about various cultures in their quest.

When we turned our attention to drugs, we immediately confronted the societal judgments and punitive consequences of drug use, which are often based on who the groups of users are. Examples throughout history vividly demonstrate the variability of a drug's fate, ranging from legal to illegal. We saw how those in charge of the science of drug use as well as those in charge of drug policy often do not share the pain of the consequences of these decisions. Even the words we choose to delineate the purposes for drug use, such as "therapeutic use" or "recreational use" or "ceremonial use," are cultural constructs.

The field of recovery is a place where an understanding of culture can potentially benefit the design and context of treatment for substance misuse. This is in many ways an untapped area of inquiry. In some of our examples, relatively easy modifications in treatment approaches, as we have seen in the case of Native smoking cessation programs, offer the potential for saving lives. Other approaches, such as 12-step programs for nicotine addiction, are yet to be tested.

We began this book by viewing the human use of substances as a kind of natural experiment in that the behaviors that surround substance use and misuse are mediated by culture, even when the substances themselves are the same. The suggested learning exercise below is a way to experience this realization firsthand.

Using Human Relations Area Files for Addictions Research

Human Relations Area Files (HRAF) are an excellent resource for conducting cross-cultural research regarding addiction and recovery. The electronic version, eHRAF, allows us to quickly scan 230 cultures throughout the world and search for information gleaned from ethnographies and other documents that have been written after long-term study of the culture. One can access eHRAF through a library that subscribes to it. A library can obtain a trial subscription to eHRAF (see http://www.yale.edu/hraf).

The ethnographies found in eHRAF are usually written in the ethnographic present, and one must be cognizant of the dates of the fieldwork. Written above the relevant paragraphs found in a eHRAF search are the dates of the fieldwork upon which the ethnography is based. One can see that there is a preponderance of older work focused on nonindustrialized societies, although eHRAF is rapidly expanding its trove to include present-day ethnographies, including those in industrialized societies.

The following are suggestions for getting started on cross-cultural research on addictions using eHRAF. There are almost an infinite number of combinations of search terms, which can be used singly or together, that will yield information from published ethnographies in cultures throughout the world. For more detailed help one can request a "webinar," wherein a professional staff person from HRAF will walk researchers through the subject/culture indexing system, the search and browse navigation, and the various search strategies.

Each ethnography has been coded according to the Outline of Cultural Materials (OCM) that consists of 710 subject categories grouped in 79 subject divisions (Ember and Ember http://www.yale.edu/hraf/guides.htm). For example, if we search for paragraphs from the 230 cultures coded by eHRAF related to drink and drugs (270) we are prompted to include eight other related categories. If we conduct a search for drink and drugs as well as alcoholic beverages (273), drinking establishments (275), pharmaceuticals (278), recreational and nontherapeutic drugs (276), and tobacco industry (277), we are led to 2,2961 paragraphs in 1,988 documents in 218 cultures. With one click we can read about our topics in ethnographies from the Akan in Africa to the Yanomamö in South America. In addition to the ethnographies of nonindustrialized countries, our search also brings us to information on alcohol, tobacco, and drug use among groups in North America, including Chinese Canadians, Hassidic Jews, Puerto Ricans of the mainland United States, Italian Americans, Arab Americans, and Haitian Americans.

We can refine our search by looking at the relationship between substances and a group or concept. For example, in order to understand more about youth, we can search the alcohol, drug, and tobacco code (270), chose all 230 cultures, and combine this with the word youth* (the asterisk will yield all variations of the word, such as youth, youths, youthful). This search will bring us 232 paragraphs in 174 documents in 96 cultures. Among the information that one will find using this search is the permissible times for Aymara adolescent girls to drink (Buechler and Buechler 1971), youth and drug use in a development town in Israel (Goldberg 1984), rules for where young men can drink in Gusii communities of Kenya (LeVine 1980), and gas sniffing and addiction in a Seminole community in Florida (Garbarino 1972).

When we search for information about efforts of abstention from alcohol in various parts of the world by combining the words abstain* and code 270 (the alcohol, drug, and tobacco code) in all 230 cultures, we find 113 paragraphs in 76 documents in 55 cultures. Among the ethnographies is a description of efforts at abstention among members of

Christian churches in the Kingdom of Tonga in the South Pacific
(Urbanowicz 1975). Once some of the members entered the "neutral"
territory of a private all-male social club, they felt free to drink alcohol
despite their pledges of abstention.

Finally, if we are trying to understand healing from a global perspective, we can combine the code 756, which is Shamans and Psycho-
therapists, with the word alcohol*. This will lead us to 50 paragraphs
in 36 documents in 25 cultures. Perhaps surprisingly, two of the ethnographies documented the concern of community members that their
medicine men were alcohol dependent, one from a Mexican-American
community (Kiev 1968) and another from an Apache community (Basso
1970). There is a description of the Medicine Men's Association within
the Navajo community efforts to establish a certification for healers
that would encourage them to confront improper conduct, including
alcohol use, during the healing ceremonies (Davies 2001). An early ethnography of a Seminole community in south Florida documents the
community's belief that the medicine man can cure an alcoholic with a
song (Sturtevant 1955).

Bibliography

"Addressing Tobacco Use in Homeless Populations: Recommendations of the Expert Panel." West Sacramento, CA: Break Free Alliance, Health Education Council. 2009. http://healthedcouncil.org/breakfreealliance/pdf/ BreakFree_TobHomelessBkltPrf3.pdf.

Agar, M. *Rippling and Running: A Formal Ethnography of Urban Heroin Addicts.* New York: Seminar Press, 1973.

"Alcohol: Balancing Risks and Benefits." Harvard School of Public Health, The Nutrition Source. 2011. http://www.hsph.harvard.edu/nutritionsource/what-should-you-eat/ alcohol-full-story/index.html#possible_health_benefits.

"Alcohol, Drug, and Tobacco Study Group Takes a Stand." Public Policy Statement. *Medical Anthropology Quarterly* 21, no. 3 (2007): 343–347.

"Alcohol and Harm Reduction in Russia." *The Lancet* 373, no. 9682 (2009): 2171.

Alcoholics Anonymous World Services Inc. *Twelve Steps and Twelve Traditions.* New York: Author, 2008.

Alegría, M. et al. "Improving Drug Treatment Services for Hispanics: Research Gaps and Scientific Opportunities." *Drug and Alcohol Dependence* 84 (September 2006): S76–S84.

Allen, C. J. *The Hold Life Has: Coca and Cultural Identity in an Andean Community.* Washington, DC and New York: Smithsonian Institution, 2002.

American Psychiatric Association. *Diagnostic and Statistical Manual of Mental Disorders, Fourth Edition, Text Revision.* Washington DC: Author, 2000.

Anderson, B. "How French Children Learn to Drink." In *Beliefs, Behaviors, & Alcoholic Beverages: A Cross Cultural Survey*, edited by Mac Marshall, 429–432. Ann Arbor: The University of Michigan Press, 1979.

Anderson, S., S. Glantz, and P. Ling. "Emotions for Sale: Cigarette Advertising and Women's Psychological Needs." *Tobacco Control* 14 (2005): 127–135.

Andrews, T. "A Family History of Alcohol Use." In *Drinking Careers: A Twenty-Five-Year Study of Three Navajo Populations*, edited by Stephen J. Kunitz and Jerold E. Levy, 139–167. New Haven, CT and London: Yale University Press, 1994.

Anthony, J., L. Warner, and R. Kessler. "Comparative Epidemiology of Dependence on Tobacco, Alcohol, Controlled Substances, and Inhalants: Basic Findings from the National Comorbidity Survey." *Experimental & Clinical Pharmacology* 2 (1994): 244–268.

Apollonio, D. E., and R. E. Malone. "Marketing to the Marginalized: Tobacco Industry Targeting of the Homeless and Mentally Ill." *Tobacco Control* 14 (2005): 409–415.

Ashenberg Straussner, S. L., ed. *Ethnocultural Factors in Substance Abuse Treatment* New York: Guilford Press, 2001.

Backstrand, J., L. Allen, E. Martinez, and G. Pelto. "Maternal Consumption of *Pulque*, a Traditional Central Mexican Alcoholic Beverage: Relationships to Infant Growth and Development." *Public Health Nutrition* 4, no. 4 (2001): 883–891.

Basso, K. *The Cibecue Apache.* New York: Holt, Rinehart and Winston, 1970. Reissue, Long Grove, IL: Waveland Press, 1986.

Beauvais, F. "American Indians and Alcohol." *Alcohol Health and Research World* 22, no. 4 (1998): 253–259.

Bezdek, M., and P. Spicer. "Maintaining Abstinence in a Northern Plains Tribe." *Medical Anthropology Quarterly* 20, no. 2 (2006): 160–181.

Black, P. "The Anthropology of Tobacco Use: Ethnographic Data and Theoretical Issues." *Journal of Anthropological Research* 40 (1984): 475–503.

Boeri, M., C. Sterk, M. Bahora, and K. Elifson. "Poly-Drug Use among Ecstasy Users: Separate, Synergistic, and Indiscriminate Patterns." *Journal of Drug Issues* 38, no. 2 (Spring, 2008): 517–541.

Borkman, T., L. Kaskutas, and P. Owen. "Contrasting and Converging Philosophies of Three Models of Alcohol/Other Drugs Treatment: Minnesota Model, Social Model, and Addiction Therapeutic Communities." *Alcoholism Treatment Quarterly* 25, no. 3 (2007): 21–37.

Bourgois, P. *In Search of Respect: Selling Crack in El Barrio.* New York: Cambridge University Press, 2008.

Bourgois, P., and J. Schonberg. *Righteous Dopefiend.* Berkeley and Los Angeles: University of California Press, 2009.

Brandes, S. *Staying Sober in Mexico City.* Austin: University of Texas Press, 2002.

Buechler, H., and J. M. Buechler. *The Bolivian Aymara.* New York: Holt, Rinehart and Winston, 1971.

Bunzel, R. "The Role of Alcoholism in Two Central American Cultures." *Psychiatry* 3 (1940): 361–387.

Burns, T. "The Rise and Fall of Assertive Community Treatment?" *International Review of Psychiatry* 22, no. 2 (2010): 130–137.

Butler, B. *Holy Intoxication to Drunken Dissipation: Alcohol among Quichua Speakers in Otavalo, Ecuador.* Albuquerque: University of New Mexico Press, 2006.

Campbell, N., and S. Shaw. "Incitements to Discourse: Illicit Drugs, Harm Reduction, and the Production of Ethnographic Subjects." *Cultural Anthropology* 23, no. 4 (2008): 688–717.

Caraballo, R. S., S. L. Yee, J. Gfroerer, and S. A. Mirza. "Adult Tobacco use among Racial and Ethnic Groups Living in the United States 2002–2005." *Preventing Chronic Disease* 5, no. 3 (2008): A78.

Caraballo, R. S., S. L. Yee, J. C. Gfroerer, T. F. Pechacek, and R. Henson. "Tobacco Use among Racial and Ethnic Population Subgroups of Adolescents in the United States." *Preventing Chronic Disease* 3, no. 2 (2006): A39

Carlson, R., M. Singer, R. Stephens, and C. Sterk. "Reflections on 40 Years of Ethnographic Drug Abuse Research: Implications for the Future." *Journal of Drug Issues* 39, no. 1 (2009): 57–70.

Carr, E. *Scripting Addiction: The Politics of Therapeutic Talk and American Sobriety.* Princeton, NJ: Princeton University Press, 2011.

CDC (Centers for Disease Control). "Highlights: Smoking among Adults in the United States: Reproductive Health." 2004. http://www.cdc.gov/tobacco/data_statistics/sgr/2004/highlights/reproductive/index.htm.

———. Press Release 2009. http://www.cdc.gov/media/pressrel/2009/r090819.htm.

———. *Tobacco Use: Targeting the Nation's Leading Killer: At a Glance.* 2009. http://www.cdc.gov/chronicdisease/resources/publications/AAG/osh.htm.

———. "Grassroots Marketing." *Designing and Implementing an Effective Tobacco Counter-Marketing Campaign*. 2010a. http://www.cdc.gov/tobacco/stateandcommunity/counter_marketing/manual/pdfs/chapter10.pdf.

———. "Health Effects of Cigarette Smoking." Fact Sheet. 2010b. http://www.cdc.gov/tobacco/data_statistics/fact_sheets/health_effects/effects_cig_smoking/.

———. "Use of Selected Substances in the Past Month among Persons 12 Years of Age and Over." *Health United States 2008*. Hyattsville, MD: CDC, 2009: 315. http://www.cdc.gov/nchs/data/hus/hus08.pdf.

Chen, K., A. Comerford, P. Shinnick, and D. Ziedonis. "Introducing Qigong Meditation into Residential Addiction Treatment: A Pilot Study Where Gender Makes a Difference." *The Journal of Alternative and Complementary Medicine* 16, no. 8 (2010): 875–882.

Cohen, P. "Medical Marijuana: The Conflict between Scientific Evidence and Political Ideology, Part Two of Two." *Journal of Pain and Palliative Care Pharmacotherapy* 23, no. 2 (2009): 120–140.

Critchlow, P. "First Steps: AA and Alcoholism in Russia." *Wilson Quarterly* 25, no. 1 (2001): 119.

Daley, C. et al. "'Tobacco Has a Purpose, Not Just a Past:' Feasibility of Developing a Culturally Appropriate Smoking Cessation Program for a Pan-Tribal Native Population." *Medical Anthropology Quarterly* 20, no. 4 (2006): 421–440.

Davies, W. *Healing Ways: Navajo Health Care in the Twentieth Century*. Albuquerque: University of New Mexico Press, 2001.

de Garine, I., and V. de Garine, eds. *Drinking: Anthropological Approaches*. New York: Berghahn Books, 2001.

Dei, K. *Ties That Bind*. Long Grove, IL: Waveland Press, 2002.

Des Jarlais, D., S. Friedman, and D. Strug. "AIDS and Needle Sharing Within the IV-Drug Use Subculture." In *Social Dimensions of AIDS: Method and Theory*, edited by Douglas A. Feldman and Thomas M. Johnson, 111–125. New York: Praeger, 1986.

Dettwyler, K. *Cultural Anthropology and the Human Experience*. Long Grove, IL: Waveland Press, 2011.

Dietler, M. "Alcohol: Anthropological/Archaeological Perspectives." *Annual Review of Anthropology* 35 (2006): 229–249.

Dougherty, J. "For Some Seeking Rebirth, Sweat Lodge Was End." *The New York Times*, October 22, 2009. http://www.nytimes.com/2009/10/22/us/22sweat.html:pagewanted=all.

Dresser, R. "Irrational Basis: The Legal Status of Medical Marijuana." *Hastings Center Report* (November–December 2009): 7–8.

Eber, C. *Women & Alcohol in a Highland Maya Town: Water of Hope, Water of Sorrow*. Austin: University of Texas Press, 2000.

Egorova, A. Personal communication about the history of AA in Russia, 2002.

Ehlers, C. "Variations in ADH and ALDH in Southwest California Indians." *Alcohol Health and Research World* 30, no. 1 (2007):14–17.

Erickson, C. K. *The Science of Addiction: From Neurobiology to Treatment*. New York: W. W. Norton, 2007.

Ernst, A. "On the Etymology of the Word Tobacco." *The American Anthropologist* Vol. II (1889): 133–142. doi: 10.1525/aa.1889.2.2.02a00020.

Frake, C. "A Structural Description of Subanun 'Religious Behavior.'" In *Explorations in Cultural Anthropology: Essays in Honor of George Peter Murdock*, edited by Ward H. Goodenough, 112. New York: McGraw-Hill, 1964.

Fagerström, K., and N. Schneider. "Measuring Nicotine Dependence: A Review of the Fagerström Tolerance Questionnaire." *Journal of Behavioral Medicine* 12: 159–181.

Ferrelly, M. et al. "Getting to the Truth: Evaluating National Tobacco Countermarketing." *American Journal of Public Health* 92, no. 6 (2002): 901–907.

Furst, P. *The Flesh of the Gods: The Ritual Use of Hallucinogens*. Westport, CT: Praeger, 1972. Reissue Long Grove, IL: Waveland Press, 1990.

Garbarino, M. *Big Cypress: A Changing Seminole Community.* New York: Holt, Rinehart and Winston, 1972.

Gladwell, M. "Drinking Games." *The New Yorker* (February 15 & 22, 2010): 70–76.

Glasser, I. *More than Bread: Ethnography of a Soup Kitchen.* Tuscaloosa: University of Alabama Press, 1988.

———. *Homelessness in Global Perspective.* New York: G. K. Hall Reference, A Division of MacMillan, 1994.

———. "Treatment of Alcohol Use Disorders in the Homeless Population." *Social Work Education for the Prevention and Treatment of Alcohol Use Disorders.* Washington, DC: National Institutes of Health, National Institute on Alcohol Abuse and Alcoholism, 2002. http://pubs.niaaa.nih.gov/publications/Social/Module10DHomeless/Module10D.html.

———. "Nicotine Anonymous May Benefit Nicotine-Dependent Individuals." Letter in response to article on cigarette use and nicotine dependence. *American Journal of Public Health* 100, no. 2 (2010): 196.

———. "AA in Russia." Poster presented at the Research Society on Alcoholism Conference, Ft. Lauderdale, FL, 2003.

Glasser, I., and R. Bridgman. *Braving the Street: The Anthropology of Homelessness.* New York: Berghahn Books, 1999.

Glasser, I., L. Fournier, and A. Costopoulos. "Homelessness in Quebec City, Quebec and Hartford, Connecticut: A Cross-National and Cross Cultural Analysis." *Urban Anthropology and Studies of Cultural Systems and World Economic Development* 28, no. 2 (1999): 141–164.

Glasser, I., and W. Zywiak. "Homelessness and Substance Use: A Tale of Two Cities." *Substance Use and Misuse* 38, no. 3–6 (Feb–May, 2003): 553–578.

Gmelch, G. *The Irish Tinkers: The Urbanization of an Itinerant People*, 2nd ed. Long Grove, IL: Waveland Press, 1985.

Goldberg, H. *Greentown's Youth: Disadvantaged Youth in a Development Town in Israel.* Assen, The Netherlands: Van Gorcum, 1984.

Gonzales, D., D. Redtomahawk, B. Pizacani, W. Bjornson, J. Spradley, E. Allen, and P. Lees. "Support for Spirituality in Smoking Cessation: Results of Pilot Survey." *Nicotine & Tobacco Research* 9, no. 2 (2007): 299–303.

Goodman, J. *Tobacco in History: The Cultures of Dependence.* London, England: Routledge, 1994.

Goodwin, R., K. Keyes, and D. Hasin. "Changes in Cigarette Use and Nicotine Dependence in the United States: Evidence from the 2001–2002 Wave of the National Epidemiologic Survey of Alcoholism and Related Conditions." *American Journal of Public Health* 99 (2009): 1471–1477.

Grim, C. "Tobacco Use in Indian Country—Issues and Opportunities." Indian Health Service Tobacco Taskforce Meeting, April 23, 2007.

Grobsmith, E. *Lakota of the Rosebud: A Contemporary Ethnography.* Fort Worth, Texas: Harcourt Brace College Publishers, 1981.

Gurdin, J. *Motherhood, Patriarchy, and the Nation: Domestic Violence in Iceland.* Iowa City: University of Iowa Press, 1996.

Hakim, D., and T. Kaplan. "As Republicans Resist Closing Prisons, Cuomo Is Said to Scale Back Plan." *The New York Times*, January 28, 2011: A19.

Hawkins, K., J. Schwartz-Thompson, and A. Kahane. "Abuse of Formaldehyde-Laced Marijuana May Cause Dysmnesia." *Journal of Neuropsychiatry and Clinical Neurosciences* 6, no. 1 (1994): 67.

Heath, D. "Drinking Patterns of the Bolivian Camba." In *Quarterly Journal of Alcohol Studies*, 19 (1958): 491–508.

———. "Alcohol and Drugs." In *Encyclopedia of Cultural Anthropology*, edited by David Levinson and Melvin Ember, 38–45. New York: Henry Holt and Company, 1996.

———. *Drinking Occasions: Comparative Perspectives on Alcohol and Culture.* Philadelphia, PA: Brunner/Mazel, 2000.

———. "Why We Don't Know More about the Social Benefits of Moderate Drinking." *Annals of Epidemiology* 17, no. 5 (2007): S71–S74.

Heath, D., and I. Glasser. "Alcohol Use." In *Encyclopedia of Medical Anthropology*, Vol.1, edited by Carol R. Ember and Melvin Ember, 293–300. New York: Kluwer/ Plenum, 2004.

Heatherton, T. F., L. T. Kozlowski, R. C. Frecker, and K. O. Fagerström. "The Fagerström Test for Nicotine Dependence: A Revision of the Fagerström Tolerance Questionnaire." *British Journal of Addictions* 86 (1991): 1119–1127.

Herlihy, P. *The Alcoholic Empire: Vodka and Politics in Late Imperial Russia*. Oxford: Oxford University Press, 2002.

Hester, R., and W. Miller. *Handbook of Alcoholism Treatment Approaches: Effective Alternatives*. Needham Heights, MA: Allyn & Bacon, 2003.

Hingson, R., and M. Winter. "Epidemiology and Consequences of Drinking and Driving." *Alcohol Research & Health* 27, no. 1 (2003): 63–78.

Hoffer, L. *Junkie Business: The Evolution and Operation of a Heroin Dealing Network*. Belmont, CA: Thompson Wadsworth, 2006.

Hoffer, L, G. Bobashev, and R. Morris. "Researching a Local Heroin Market as a Complex Adaptive System." *American Journal of Community Psychology* 44 (2009): 273–286.

Hume, L. *Portals: Opening Doorways to Other Realities through the Senses*. Oxford, UK: Berg, 2007.

Humphreys, K. *Circles of Recovery: Self-Help Organizations for Addictions*. Cambridge, UK: Cambridge University Press, 2004.

Humphreys, K. "Professional Interventions That Facilitate 12-Step Self-Help Group Involvement" *Alcohol Research and Health* 23, no. 2 (1999): 93–98.

Hunt, G., and J. Barker. "Drug Treatment in Contemporary Anthropology and Sociology." *European Addiction Research* 5 (1999):126–132.

Hunt, G., M. Moloney, and K. Evans. "Epidemiology Meets Cultural Studies: Studying and Understanding Youth Cultures, Clubs and Drugs." *Addiction Research and Theory* 17, no 6 (2009): 601–621.

Hyde, G. *Spotted Tail's Folk: A History of the Brule Sioux*. Norman: University of Oklahoma Press, 1961.

Jacinto, C., M. Duterte, P. Sales, and S. Murphy. "'I'm Not a Real Dealer': The Identity Process of Ecstasy Sellers." *Journal of Drug Issues* 38, no. 2 (2008): 419–444.

Jarvenpa, R. *Northern Passage: Ethnography and Apprenticeship among the Subarctic Dene*. Long Grove, IL: Waveland Press, 1998.

Johnson, J., J. Bottorffa, B. Moffat, P. Ratnerb, J. Shovellerc, and C. Lovatec. "Tobacco Dependence: Adolescents' Perspectives on the Need to Smoke." *Social Science and Medicine* 56, no. 7 (2003): 1481–1492.

Jones, P. "The Native American Church, Peyote, and Health: Expanding Consciousness for Healing Purposes." *Contemporary Justice Review* 10, no. 4 (2007): 411–425.

Joseph, A., R. Spicer., and J. Chesky. *The Desert People: A Study of the Papago Indians*. Chicago: University of Chicago Press, 1949.

Kagan, H., and K. C. Shafer. "Russian-Speaking Substance Abusers in Transition." In *Ethnocultural Factors in Substance Abuse Treatment*, edited by Shulmith Lala Ashenberg Straussner. New York: The Guilford Press, 2001.

Kandel, D., L. Adler, and M. Sudit. "The Epidemiology of Adolescent Drug Use in France and Israel." *American Journal of Public Health* 7, no. 3 (1981): 256–265.

Kaskutas, L. "Alcoholics Anonymous Effectiveness: Faith Meets Science." *Journal of Addictive Diseases* 28, no. 2 (2009): 145–157.

Kearney, M. "Drunkenness and Religious Conversion in a Mexican Village." *Quarterly Studies on Alcohol* 31 (1970): 132–152.

Kearney, M. *The Winds of Ixtepeji: Worldview and Society in a Zapotec Town*. Long Grove, IL: Waveland Press, 1986.

Keller, M. "The Great Jewish Drink Mystery." In *Beliefs, Behaviors, & Alcoholic Beverages: A Cross Cultural Survey*, edited by Mac Marshall, 401–414. Ann Arbor: The University of Michigan Press, 1979.

Kiev, A. *Curanderismo: Mexican-American Folk Psychiatry.* New York: Free Press, 1968.

Kunitz, S., and J. Levy. *Drinking Careers: A Twenty-Five-Year Study of Three Navajo Populations.* New Haven, CT and London: Yale University Press, 1994.

La Barre, W. *The Peyote Cult*, 5th ed. Norman: University of Oklahoma Press, 1989.

Lankenau, S. "Smoke 'Em If You Got 'Em: Cigarette Black Markets in U.S. Prisons and Jails." *The Prison Journal* 81, no. 2 (2001): 142–161.

Lasser, K., J. W. Boyd, and S. Woolhandler. "Smoking and Mental Illness: A Population-Based Prevalence Study." *JAMA* 284, no. 20 (2000): 2606–2610.

Lende, D., T. Leonard, C. Sterk, and K. Elifson. "Functional Methamphetamine Use: The Insider's Perspective." *Addiction Research and Theory* 15, no. 5 (October, 2007): 465–477.

Leppel, K. "College Binge Drinking: Deviant Versus Mainstream Behavior." *The American Journal of Drug and Alcohol Abuse* 32 (2006): 519–525.

LeVine, R. "Adulthood among the Gusii of Kenya." In *Themes of Work and Love in Adulthood*, edited by Neil J. Smelser and Erik H. Erikson, 77–104. Cambridge, MA: Harvard University Press, 1980.

Lewis, S. "Ayahuasca and Spiritual Crisis: Liminality as Space for Personal Growth." *Anthropology of Consciousness* 19, no. 2 (2008): 109–133.

Lichtenstein, E. "Nicotine Anonymous: Community Resource and Research Implications." *Psychology of Addictive Behaviors* 13, no. 1 (1999): 60–68.

Liddle, H. A., C. L. Rowe, C. E. Henderson, G. A. Dakof, and P. E. Greenbaum. "Multidimensional Family Therapy for Young Adolescent Substance Abuse: Twelve-Month Outcomes of a Randomized Controlled Trial." *Journal of Consulting and Clinical Psychology* 77, no. 1 (2009): 12–25.

Luciano, P. A., J. L. Sotheran, and M. C. Clatts. "The Geography of an Unsafe Injection: IV Drug Use and Commercial Sex Workers." *Practicing Anthropology* 22, no. 2 (2000): 33–32.

Lurigio, A., and P. Loose. "The Disproportionate Incarceration of African Americans for Drug Offenses: The National and Illinois Perspective." *Journal of Ethnicity in Criminal Justice* 6, no. 3 (2008): 223–247.

MacAndrew, C., and R. Edgerton. *Drunken Comportment: A Social Explanation.* Clinton Corners, NY: Percheron Press, 2003.

Madsen, W., and C. Madsen. "The Cultural Structure of Mexican Drinking Behavior." In *Beliefs, Behaviors, & Alcoholic Beverages: A Cross Cultural Survey*, edited by Mac Marshall, 38–54. Ann Arbor: The University of Michigan Press, 1979.

Mäkelä, K. et al. *Alcoholics Anonymous as a Mutual-Help Movement: A Study in Eight Societies* Madison: University of Wisconsin Press, 1996.

Manghi, R. A., B. Broers, R. Khan, D. Benguettat, Y. Khazaal, and D. Zulino. "Khat Use: Lifestyle or Addiction?" *Journal of Psychoactive Drugs* 41, no. 1 (2009): 1–10.

Marr-Lyon, L., K. Young, and G. Quintero. "An Evaluation of Youth Empowerment Tobacco Prevention Programs in the Southwest." *Journal of Drug Education* 38, no. 1 (2008): 39–53.

Marshall, M., ed. *Beliefs, Behaviors, & Alcoholic Beverages: A Cross Cultural Survey.* Ann Arbor: The University of Michigan Press, 1979a.

——. *Weekend Warriors: Alcoholism in a Micronesian Culture.* Palo Alto, CA: Mayfield, 1979b.

——. "Carolina in the Carolines: A Survey of Patterns and Meanings of Smoking on a Micronesian Island." *Medical Anthropology Quarterly* 19, no. 4 (2005): 365–382.

Marshall, M., G. Ames, and L. A. Bennett. "Anthropological Perspectives on Alcohol and Drugs at the Turn of the New Millennium." *Social Science and Medicine* 53, no. 2 (2001): 153–164.

Martin, J. E., K. J. Calfas, C. A. Patten, M. Polarek, C. R. Hofstetter, J. Noto, and D. Beach. "Prospective Evaluation of Three Smoking Interventions in 205 Recovering Alcoholics: One-Year Results of Project SCRAP-Tobacco." *Journal of Consulting and Clinical Psychology* 65 (1997): 190–194.

May, P. A., J. P. Gossage, L. E. Brooke, et al. "Maternal Risk Factors for Fetal Alcohol Syndrome in the Western Cape Province of South Africa: A Population-Based Study." *American Journal of Public Health* 95 (2005): 1190–1199.

McElroy, A., and P. Townsend. *Medical Anthropology in Ecological Perspective*, 5th ed. Boulder CO: Westview Press, 2009.

McGill, D. "Cigarette Industry Financing Wide War on Smoking Bans." *New York Times*, December 24, 1988. http://www.nytimes.com/1988/12/24/business/cigarette-industry-financing-wide-war-on-smoking-bans.html?pagewanted=all&src=pm.

McKellar, J., E. Stewart, and K. Humphreys. "Alcoholics Anonymous Involvement and Positive Alcohol-Related Outcomes: Cause, Consequence, or Just a Correlate? A Prospective 2-Year Study of 2,319 Alcohol Dependent Men." *Journal of Consulting and Clinical Psychology* 71, no. 2 (2003): 302–308.

McKnight, D. *From Hunting to Drinking; The Devastating Effects of Alcohol on an Australian Aboriginal Community.* London: Routledge, 2002.

Medicine, B. *Drinking and Sobriety among the Lakota Sioux.* Lanham, MD: Altamira Press, 2007.

Merriam-Webster Online Dictionary. Central nervous system. 2010.

"Mescaline—The Law." In *Encyclopedia of Drugs and Addictive Substances*, edited by Barbara C. Bigelow. Gale Cengage, eNotes.com. 2006. http://www.enotes.com/drugs-substances-encyclopedia/mescaline/law.

"Methamphetamine Laboratories." Illinois Department of Public Health Environmental Fact Sheet. n.d. http://www.idph.state.il/us/envhealth/factsheets/meth-labs.htm.

Mignon, S., M. Faiia, P. Myers, and E. Rubington. *Substance Use & Abuse: Exploring Alcohol and Drug Issues.* Boulder CO: Lynne Rienner, 2009.

Moerman, D. "Cultural Variations in the Placebo Effect: Ulcers, Anxiety, and Blood Pressure." *Medical Anthropology Quarterly* 14, no. 1 (2000): 51–72.

Moffat, M. *Coming of Age in New Jersey: College and American Life.* New Brunswick, NJ: Rutgers University Press, 1989.

Moore, L., and A. Elkavich. "Who's Using and Who's Doing Time: Incarceration, the War on Drugs, and Public Health." *American Journal of Public Health* 98, Supplement 1 (September 2008): S176–S180.

Moore, R., R. Annechino, and J. Lee. "Unintended Consequences of Smoke-Free Bar Policies for Low-SES Women in Three California Counties." *American Journal of Preventive Medicine* 37, Supplement 2 (August, 2009): S138–S142.

Morrow, M., D. H. Ngoc, R. R. Hoang, and T. H. Trinh. "Smoking and Young Women in Vietnam: The Influence of Normative Gender Roles." *Social Science and Medicine* 55 (2002): 681–690.

National Center for Health Statistics. *Health, United States, 2010: With Special Feature on Death and Dying.* Hyattsville, MD: Author, 2011.

National Survey on Drug Use and Health "Trends in Tobacco Use among Adolescents: 2002–2008." October 15, 2009. http://oas.samhsa.gov/2k9/152/152Trends.htm.

NIAAA (National Institute on Alcohol Abuse and Alcoholism). "New Advances in Alcoholism Treatment." *Alcohol Alert* no. 49. 2000. http://publs.niaaa.nih.gov/publications/aa49.htm.

NIDA. Research Report Series—Prescription Medications. 2005. http://www.nida.nih.gov/PDF/RRPrescription.pdf.

———. InfoFacts "Hallucinogens—LSD, Peyote, Psilocybin, and PCP." 2009a. http://www.drugabuse.gov/infofacts/hallucinogens.html.

———. "Treatment Approaches for Drug Addiction." 2009b. http://www.nida.nih.gov/PDF/InfoFacts/IF_Treatment_Approaches_2009_to_NIDA_92209.pdf.

———. Research Report Series—Heroin Abuse and Addiction. 2010a. http://www.nida.nih.gov/PDF/RRHeroin.pdf.

———. "Commonly Abused Drugs." 2010b. http://www.drugabuse.gov/DrugPages/DrugsofAbuse.html.

———. Research Report Series—Marijuana Abuse. 2010c. http://www.nida.nih.gov/PDF/RRMarijuana.pdf.

———. InfoFacts "Cocaine." 2010d. http://www.nida.nih.gov/infofacts/cocaine.html.

———. InfoFacts: Methamphetamine. 2010e. http://www.nida.nih.gov/infofacts/methamphetmine.html.

———. InfoFacts "Khat." 2011. http://www.nida.nih.gov/Infofacts/khat.html.

———. "Tobacco/Nicotine." n.d. http://www.nida.nih.gov/drugpages/nicotine.html.

Nichter, M., S. Padmawati, M. Danardono, N. Ng, Y. Prabandani, and M. Nichter. "Reading Culture from Tobacco Advertisements in Indonesia." *Tobacco Control* 18 (2009): 98–107.

Nichter, M., M. Nichter, M. Muramoto, et al. "Smoking among Low-Income Pregnant Women: An Ethnographic Analysis." *Health Education and Behavior* 34, no. 5 (2007): 748–764.

Nichter, M., M. Nichter, N. Vuckovic, L. Tesher, S. Adrion, and C. Ritenbaugh. "Smoking as a Weight Control Strategy among Adolescent Girls and Young Women: A Reconsideration." *Medical Anthropology Quarterly* 18, no. 3 (2004): 305–324.

Norton, M. *Sacred Gifts, Profane Pleasures.* Ithaca, NY: Cornell University Press, 2008.

Padgett, D., L. Gulcur, and S. Tsemberis. "Housing First Services for People Who Are Homeless With Co-Occurring Serious Mental Illness and Substance Abuse." *Research on Social Work Practice* 16 (2006):74–83.

Page, J. B. "Drug Use." In *Encyclopedia of Medical Anthropology,* Vol. 1 edited by Carol R. Ember and Melvin Ember, 374-382. New York: Kluwer/Plenum, 2004.

Page, J. B., D. Chitwood, P. Smith, N. Kane, and D. McBride. "Intravenous Drug Use and HIV Infection in Miami." *Medical Anthropology Quarterly* 4, no. 1 (1990): 56–71.

Page, J. B., and M. Singer. *Comprehending Drug Use: Ethnographic Research at the Social Margins.* New Brunswick, NJ: Rutgers University Press, 2010.

Paper, J. *Native North American Religious Traditions: Dancing for Life* Westport, CT: Praeger, 2007.

Pathania, V. S. "Women and the Smoking Epidemic: Turning the Tide." *Bulletin of the World Health Organization* 89 (2011): 162. doi: 10.2471/BLT.11.08639. http://www.who.int/bulletin/volumes/89/3/11-086389/en/index.html.

Pollard, N. "UN Report Puts World's Illicit Drug Trade at Estimated $321B." *Boston Globe,* June 30, 2005. http://www.boston.com/news/world/europe/articles/2005/06/30/un_report_puts_worlds_illicit_drug_trade_at_estimated_321b/.

Preble, E., and J. Casey. "Taking Care of Business: The Heroin User's Life on the Street." *International Journal of the Addictions* 4, no. 1 (1969): 1–24.

Project Match Research Group. "Project Match and Methods for a Multisite Clinical Trial Matching Patients to Alcoholism Treatment." *Alcohol and Experimental Research* 17 (1993): 1130–1145.

Quintero, G., and S. Davis. "Why Do Teens Smoke? American Indian and Hispanic Adolescents' Perspectives on Functional Values and Addiction." *Medical Anthropology Quarterly* 16, no. 4 (2002): 439–457.

Quintero, G., J. Peterson, and B. Young. "An Exploratory Study of Socio-Cultural Factors Contributing to Prescription Drug Misuse among College Students." *Journal of Drug Issues* 36, no. 4 (Fall, 2006): 903–993.

Quintero, G., K. Young, N. Nier, and S. Jenks. "Perceptions of Drinking Among Hispanic College Students: How Qualitative Research Can Inform the Development of Collegiate Alcohol Abuse Prevention Programs." *Journal of Drug Education* 35, no. 4 (2005): 291–304.

Rhoades, D., E. Rhoades, C. Jones, and R. Collins. *Tobacco Use in American Indian Health: Innovations in Health Care, Promotion, and Policy*, edited by Everett R. Rhoades. Baltimore, MD: The Johns Hopkins University Press, 2000.

Richburg, K. B. "As Census Nears, How to Count Inmates Is Debated." *Washington Post*, April 26, 2009. http://www.washingtonpost.com/wp-dyn/content/article/2009/04/25/AR2009042501403.html.

Richter, P., D. Beistle, L. Pederson, and M. O'Hegarty. "Small-Group Discussions on Menthol Cigarettes: Listening to Adult African American Smokers in Atlanta, Georgia." *Ethnicity and Health* 13, no. 2 (2008): 171–182.

Rodu, B., and P. Cole. "Declining Mortality from Smoking in the United States." *Nicotine and Tobacco Research* 9, no. 7 (2007): 781–784.

Rogers, E. M. *Diffusion of Innovation*, 4th ed. New York: The Free Press, 1995.

"Room for Debate Blog: If Marijuana Is Legal, Will Addiction Rise?" *New York Times* (July 19, 2009).

Samet, J. M. "Health Effects of Tobacco Use by Native North Americans: Past and Present." In *Tobacco Use by Native North Americans: Sacred Smoke and Silent Killer*, edited by Joseph C. Winter. Norman: University of Oklahoma Press, 2000: 311–341.

SAMHSA. *Guiding Principles and Elements of Recovery Oriented Systems of Care: What Do We Know from the Research?* Rockville, MD: Center for Substance Abuse Treatment, Substance Abuse and Mental Health Services Administration (SAMHSA), 2009. http://pfr.samhsa.gov/docs/Guiding_Principles_Whitepaper.pdf.

Saris, A. "An Uncertain Dominion: Irish Psychiatry, Methadone, and the Treatment of Opiate Abuse." *Culture, Medicine, and Psychiatry* 32 (2008): 259–277.

Saunders, J. "Substance Dependence and Non-Dependence." In *Diagnostic and Statistical Manual of Mental Disorders* (DSM) and the *International Classification of Diseases* (ICD): Can an identical conceptualization be achieved?" *Addiction* 101, Suppl. 1: 48–58.

Saunders, N., A. Saunders, and M. Pauli. *In Search of the Ultimate High: Spiritual Experiences through Psychoactives*. London: Rider, 2000.

Sexton, R., R. Carlson, C. Leukefeld, and B. Booth. "Methamphetamine Use and Adverse Consequences in the Rural Southern United States: An Ethnographic Overview." *Journal of Psychoactive Drugs* 38, SARC Supplement 3 (2006, November): 393–404.

Singer, M. *Something Dangerous: Emergent and Changing Illicit Drug Use and Community Health*. Long Grove, IL: Waveland Press, 2006a.

———. *The Face of Social Suffering: The Life History of a Street Drug Addict*. Long Grove, IL: Waveland Press, 2006b.

———. *Drugs and Development: The Global Impact on Sustainable Growth and Human Rights*. Long Grove, IL: Waveland Press, 2008.

Singer, M., J. Juvalis, and M. Weeks. "High on Illy: Monitoring an Emergent Drug Problem in Hartford, CT." *Medical Anthropology*, 18, no. 4 (2000): 365–388.

Singer, M., F. Valentín, H. Baer, and Z. Jia. "Why Does Juan García Have a Drinking Problem? The Perspective of Critical Medical Anthropology." *Medical Anthropology* 14, no. 1 (1992): 77–108.

Skoll, G. *Talk the Walk and Talk the Talk*. Philadelphia: Temple University Press, 1992.

Skorpen, A., N. Anderssen, C. Oeye, and A. Bjelland. "The Smoking-Room as Psychiatric Patients' Sanctuary: A Place for Resistance." *Journal of Psychiatric and Mental Health Nursing* 15 (2008): 728–736.

Smith, E., K. Thomson, N. Offen, and R. Malone. "'If You Know You Exist, It's Just Marketing Poison': Meanings of Tobacco Industry Targeting in the Lesbian, Gay, Bisexual, and Transgender Community." *American Journal of Public Health* 98, no. 6 (2008): 996–1003.

Smith, F. *Caribbean Rum: A Social and Economic History*. Gainesville: University Press of Florida, 2005.

———. *The Archeology of Alcohol and Drinking*. Gainesville: University Press of Florida, 2008.

Spradley, J. *You Owe Yourself a Drunk: An Ethnography of Urban Nomads*. Boston: Little, Brown, 1970. Reissue, Long Grove, IL: Waveland Press, 2000.

Stahler, G., and E. Cohen. "Using Ethnographic Methodology in Substance Abuse Treatment Outcome Research." *Journal of Substance Abuse Treatment* 18 (2000): 1–8.

Stahler, G., T. Shipley, D. Bartelt, J. DuCette, and I. Shandler. "Evaluating Alternative Treatment for Homeless Substance-Abusing Men: Outcomes and Predictors of Success." *Journal of Addictive Diseases* 14 (1995): 151–167.

Sterk, C. *Fast Lives: Women Who Use Crack Cocaine* Philadelphia, PA: Temple University Press, 1999.

Stromberg, P., M. Nichter, and M. Nichter. "Taking Play Seriously: Low-Level Smoking among College Students." *Culture, Medicine and Psychiatry* 31 (2007): 1–24.

Sturtevant, W. *The Mikasuki Seminole: Medical Beliefs and Practices*. Ann Arbor, MI: University Microfilms International, 1989 copy. v, 539.

Swora, M. "The Rhetoric of Transformation in the Healing of Alcoholism: The Twelve Steps of Alcoholics Anonymous." *Mental Health, Religion & Culture* 7, no. 3 (2004): 187–209.

The Moscow Times. "Alcoholics Anonymous Sheds Some Anonymity," July 15, 2005. http://www.themoscowtimes.com/news/article.

Trevor, W. *After Rain*. London, UK: Penguin Books, 1996.

Turner, V. *The Ritual Process: Structure and Anti-Structure*. Chicago: Aldine, 1969.

2010 National Survey on Drug Use and Health: US Department of Health and Human Services. http://oas.samhsa.gov/NSDUH/2k10NSDUH/2k10Results.htm#5.5.

Underhill, R. *Papago Woman*. Long Grove, IL: Waveland Press, 1985.

———. *Singing for Power: The Song Magic of the Papago Indians of Southern Arizona*. Berkeley: The University of California Press, 1938.

Urbanowicz, C. "Drinking in the Polynesian Kingdom of Tonga." *Ethnohistory* 22, no. 1 (1975): 33–50.

U.S. Drug Enforcement Administration, "Khat." n.d. http://www.justice.gov/dea/concern/khat.html.

"Vienna Declaration." 2010. http://www.viennadeclaration.com.

Volkow, N. "Testimony Scientific Research on Prescription Drug Abuse." 2008. http://www.hhs.gov/asl/testify/2008/03/t20080312a.html.

von Gernet, A "North American Indigenous Nicotiana Use and Tobacco Shamanism." In *Tobacco Use by Native North Americans: Sacred Smoke and Silent Killer*, edited by J. Winter. Norman: University of Oklahoma Press, 2000.

Wakefield, M. et al. "Effect of Televised, Tobacco Company-Funded Smoking Prevention Advertising on Youth Smoking-Related Beliefs, Intentions and Behaviors." *American Journal of Public Health* 96, no. 12 (2006): 2154–2160.

Waldram, J. *The Way of the Pipe: Aboriginal Spirituality and Symbolic Health in Canadian Prisons*. Peterborough, Ontario: Broadview Press, 1997.

Waterston, A. *Love, Sorrow, and Rage: Destitute Women in a Manhattan Residence*. Philadelphia, PA: Temple University Press, 1999.

Wechsler, H. *Binge Drinking on America's College Campuses: Findings from the Harvard School of Public Health College Alcohol Study*. 2000. Monograph. www.hspsh.harvard.edu/cas/Documents/monograph_2000/cas/mono_2000.pdf.

Wechsler, H., and T. Nelson. "What We Have Learned From the Harvard School of Public Health College Alcohol Study: Focusing Attention on College Student Alcohol Consumption and the Environmental Conditions That Promote It." *Journal of Studies on Alcohol and Drugs* 69 no. 4 (July, 2008): 481–490.

Wellin, E. "Water Boiling in a Peruvian Town." In *Health, Culture and Community*, edited by B. Paul, 71–102. New York: Russell Sage Foundation 1955.

Wewers, M. E., M. Katz, D. Fickle, and E. D. Paskett. "Risky Behaviors among Ohio Appalachian Adults." *Preventing Chronic Disease: Public Health Research, Practice, and Policy* 3, no. 4 (2006): 1–8.

"When Don't Smoke Means Do." *New York Times*, Nov. 27, 2006. http://www.nytimes.com/2006/11/27/opinion/27mon1.html.

White, W. "Recovery: Old Wine, Flavor of the Month, or New Organizing Paradigm?" *Substance Use & Misuse* 43 (2008):1987–2000.

White, W. "The Rhetoric of Recovery Advocacy: An Essay on the Power of Language." 2011. http://www.bhrm.org/advocacy/rhetoric.pdf.

Whitten, L. "Studies Identify Factors Surrounding Rise in Abuse of Prescription Drugs by College Students." *NIDA Notes* 20, no. 4 (March, 2006). http://archives.drugabuse.gov/NIDA_notes/NNvol20N4/Studies.html.

Whitworth, A., F. and Fischer. "Comparison of Acamprosate and Placebo in Long-Term Treatment of Alcohol Dependence." *The Lancet* 347, no. 9013 (1996): 1438–1450.

Wilbert, J. *Tobacco and Shamanism in South America.* New Haven, CT: Yale University Press, 1987.

Winter, J. C. "From Earth Mother to Snake Woman: The Role of Tobacco in the Evolution of Native American Religious Organizations." In *Tobacco Use by Native North Americans: Sacred Smoke and Silent Killer*, edited by J. C. Winter, 265–304. Norman: University of Oklahoma Press, 2000.

Wolcott, H. *Ethnography: A Way of Seeing.* Lanham, MD: Altamira Press, 2008.

Wood, E., et al. "Vienna Declaration: A Call for Evidence-Based Drug Policies." *The Lancet* 376 (July 2010). www.thelancet.com.

World Drink Trends. Henley-on-Thames, Oxfordshire, England: NTC Publications, 2000.

Worldwide BAC Limits. http://www.drinkdriving.org/worldwide_drink_driving_limits.php.

Yardley, W. "Violence Prompts Marijuana Debate." *The New York Times* March 16, 2010. http://www.nytimes.com/2010/03/17/us/17marijuana.html.

Young, D., G. Ingram, and L. Swartz. *Cry of the Eagle.* Toronto: University of Toronto Press, 1989.

Zerger, S. "A Look at Smoking and Homelessness." 2009. http://homeless.samhsa.gov/Resource/R2P.

Zerger, S. "Substance Abuse Treatment: What Works for Homeless People? A Review of the Literature." National Health Care for the Homeless Council, 2002.

Ziker, J. P. *Peoples of the Tundra: Native Siberians in the Post Communist Transition.* Long Grove, IL: Waveland Press, 2002.

Websites

American Anthropological Association: http://www.aa.org

Campaign for Tobacco-Free Kids: http://www.tobaccofreekids.org

Centers for Disease Control: http://www.cdc.gov

Country Profiles—The Russian Federation: http://www.who.int/substance_abuse/publications/en/russian_federation.pdf

Drug Enforcement Administration, Khat: http://www.justice.gov/dea/concern/khat.html

Health Canada: http://www.hc-sc.gc.ca

Human Relations Area Files: http://www.yale.edu/hraf

The ICD-10 Classification of Mental and Behavioural Disorders: Clinical descriptions and diagnostic guidelines: http://www.who.int/substance_abuse/terminology/ICD10ClinicalDiagnosis.pdf

Jewish Alcoholics, Chemically Dependent Persons, and Significant Others: http://www.jacsweb.org

National Institute on Drug Abuse: http://www.nida.nih.gov

National Institutes of Health: http://www.nih.gov

National Institute on Alcohol Abuse and Alcoholism: http://www.niaaa.nih.gov
Nicotine Anonymous: http://www.nicotine-anonymous.org
Rethinking Drinking—Alcohol and Your Health:
    http://www.rethinkingdrinking.niaaa.nih.gov
World Health Organization—Management of Substance Abuse: http://www.who.int/
    substance_abuse/terminology/definition2/en/index.html

Index

Aboriginal spirituality, symbolic healing through, 88–89
Addiction(s)
  behavioral, pharmacological, and residential treatment of, 77
  definition of, 5
  meditation approach to (native/indigenous), 89
  research, using Human Relations Area Files in, 98–100
African Americans
  beliefs about smoking, 41
  drug-related incarceration rates for, 60
  rates of illicit drug use among, 59
Agar, Michael, 71
AIDS/HIV. See HIV/AIDS
Alcohol
  abuse, costs of, 27–28
  Blood Alcohol Concentration (BAC), legal limits of, 9–10
  college drinking, 28–31
  cross-cultural examples of drinking, 18–21
  culture and drinking behavior, 31–32
  culture change and, 23–25

drink as food, 26–27
drinking careers, 25
drinking patterns, 25–27
driving and drinking, 27–29
ethnographic studies of, 5–8
homelessness and, 28
legal status of, 10–11
methods of introduction into communities, 21–23
moderate drinking, 26
physiological effects of, 8–10
pregnancy and drinking, 21
solitary drinking, 26, 32
use in worship, 6
See also Drinking
Alcoholics Anonymous, 79–85
  12 traditions of, 80–81
  12-step program in, 79–80, 84–85
  cultural malleability of, 82
  efficacy of, 83–85
  lack of diffusion, 85–87
Allen, Catherine, 53, 54
American Psychiatric Association's Diagnostic and Statistical Manual of Mental Disorders (DSM-IV), 12, 15–16

Amerindians. See Native Americans
Anderson, Barbara Gallatin, 26–27
Anderson, S., 42
Annechino, R., 49
Anthony, J., 10
Antismoking advertising by tobacco companies, 47
Apollonio, D. E., 48
Ashenberg Straussner, Shulamith, 92
Assertive Community Treatment (ACT), 77
Ayahuasca, 54–55

Backstrand, J., 27
Barker, Judith, 76
Binge drinking, 30–31
Boeri, Miriam, 63, 64
Bourgois, Philippe, 2–3, 67, 69–70
Brandes, Stanley, 81
Bunzel, Ruth, 5, 6

Campbell, Nancy, 70, 71
Caraballo, Ralph, 41
Casey, John, Jr., 70
Chesky, J., 24
Chitwood, D., 71
Cigarettes
  African American beliefs about, 41
  as currency, 40–41

health consequences of
smoking, 39
large profits from sale
of, 38
link with mental illness
and homelessness,
48–49
origin of, 37
smoking as play, 46
women, smoking
among, 42–43
Club drugs, 62–65
Coca leaves/cocaine, 53
Cocaine, crack, 67–68
College students
drinking among, 28–31
prescription drug use
among, 65–66
Comprehensive Drug
Abuse Prevention and
Control Act, 10
Controlled substances,
government categori-
zation/schedule of,
10–11
Costopoulos, A., 28
Crack cocaine, 67–68
Critchlow, P., 86
Culture(s)
drinking behavior and,
31–32
emic/insider categories
within, 7–8
ethnographic descrip-
tion of, 3
recovery as expression
of, 75–96

Daley, Christine, 90
Davis, S., 45
de Garine, Igor, 3
de Garine, Valerie, 3
Dei, Kojo, 68, 69
Depressants, 65
Depressants, definition of,
9
Diagnostic classification
systems, 12–13
Dietler, Michael, 32
Drinking. *See* Alcohol
Drugs
club drugs, 62–65
decriminalization/legal-
ization of, 55, 58–59,
62
dependence liability of,
10

diagnostic classification
systems for, 12–13
drug laws as cultural
artifacts, 55–59
drug policies and HIV,
62
ethnographic studies of,
5–8, 67–69
ethnography of suffer-
ing, 69–70
government categories
of controlled sub-
stances, 10–11
HIV/AIDS-related, eth-
nographic research
on, 70–71
impact of law enforce-
ment and incarcera-
tion on use of,
59–62
indiscriminate-use pat-
terns, 64
initiation/continued
participation in use
of, 67–69
international drug
trade, 60–62
legal status of, 10–11
mind-altering, indige-
nous uses of, 51–55
new, ethnographic
research on monitor-
ing, 72
pharmacological defini-
tion of, 8
physiological effects of,
8–10
polydrug use, 63–64
prescription, 65–66
synergistic use, 64
Western moralism and,
55
See also individual drug
names

Eber, Christine, 20
Ecstasy, 3, 64
Edgerton, Robert, 5, 17, 24
Egorova, A., 86
Elifson, K., 63
Elkavich, A., 59, 60
Emic categorizations, 7–8,
19
Entheogens, 54
Erickson, Carlton, 8, 9, 10,
11, 21
Ernst, Adolfo, 36

Ethnography
definition of, 3
studies of alcohol,
tobacco, and drugs,
5–8

Fetal alcohol spectrum dis-
order, 21
Fournier, L., 28
Frake, Charles, 3
Furst, Peter, 52

GHB, 63
Glantz, S., 42
Glasser, Irene, 28, 40, 86,
92
Gmelch, George, 23–24
Gmelch, Sharon, 24
Goodman, Jordan, 35, 36,
37, 38
Grobsmith, Elizabeth, 52,
53, 89

Hallucinogenic mushrooms,
52
Harrison Narcotic Act of
1914, 55
Healing
aboriginal/indigenous,
88–89
finding a global per-
spective on, 100
recovery approaches
involving, 76
transformative rhetoric
of, 84
Heath, Dwight, 18
Herlihy, Patricia, 86
Heroin, 56, 69–70
Hingson, Ralph, 9
Hispanics
adolescent smoking
among, 44–45
alcohol use rates for,
29
compadrazgo/sponsor-
ship tradition in AA,
81–82
drug-related incarcera-
tion rates for, 60
HIV/AIDS
drug policy regarding,
62
transmission through
injection drug use, 7,
70–71
Hoang, R. R., 43

Homelessness
    alcohol abuse and, 28
    as exclusion criterion in
        treatment efficacy
        studies, 4
    intervention/outreach
        treatment for home-
        less people, 92–93
    tobacco use and, 48
Human Relations Area
    Files, use in addic-
    tions research, 98–100
Hume, Lynne, 54, 55
Humphreys, Keith, 81, 83
Hunt, Geoffrey, 63, 76
Hyde, G., 22

Iatrogenic disease, 56, 69
Illy, 72
Indigenous healing, 87–89
Injection
Injection drug use/users
    drug policies impact-
        ing, 62
    ethnography of suffer-
        ing, 69–70
    HIV/AIDS transmis-
        sion through, 70–71
    increased risk of infec-
        tion from, 9, 11
    strategies of harm
        reduction, 70–71
International Classifica-
    tion of Diseases (ICD-
    10), 12, 14–15
Interventions, behavioral vs.
    pharmacologic, 77–78

Jacinto, Camille, 3
Jewish Alcoholics, Chemi-
    cally Dependent Per-
    sons, and Significant
    Others (JACS), 82–83
Jones, Peter, 52
Joseph, A., 24
Juvalis, J., 72

Kagan, H., 86
Kane, N., 71
Kaskutas, Lee Ann, 84
Kearney, Michael, 19
Keller, Mark, 26
Kessler, R., 10
Ketamine, 63
Khat, 57
Kilpatrick, Jean, 83
Kunitz, Stephen, 25

Lankenau, Stephen, 40
Lee, J., 49
Leppel, Karen, 31
Levy, Jerrold, 25
Lewis, Sara, 55
Ling, P., 42

MacAndrew, Craig, 5, 17,
    24
Madsen, Claudia, 18–19
Madsen, William, 18–19
Mäkelä, K., 82
Malone, R. E., 48
Manghi, R. A., 57
Marijuana, 57–59
Marshall, Mac, 22–23,
    31–32, 37–38
May, P. A., 21
Mayan communities, drink-
    ing in, 6, 20
McBride, D., 71
Medicine, Beatrice, 21
Mescaline, 52
Methamphetamine, 63–65
Moerman, Daniel, 78
Moffat, Michael, 29, 30
Moore, L., 59, 60
Moore, Roland, 49
Morphine, 56
Morrow, M., 43
Multidimensional family
    therapy, 78
Mutual help organizations,
    79–85

Native Americans
    aboriginal healing prac-
        tices of, 88–89
    adolescent smoking
        among, 44–45
    peyote use among,
        52–53
    rate of alcohol-related
        deaths among, 22
    smoking cessation pro-
        grams for, 90
    tobacco use among,
        36–37, 39
Nelson, T., 30
Ngoc, D. H., 43
Nichter, Mark, 46
Nichter, Mimi, 42, 46
Nicotine, 10, 43–44
Nicotine Anonymous pro-
    gram, lack of diffusion
    of, 87
Norton, Marcy, 37

Opiates, 55–56, 65

Page, J. Bryan, 7, 51, 55,
    71, 76
Participant-observation, 3
Peyote, 11, 52, 77–78
Placebos, effect in various
    world cultures, 77–78
Political economy explana-
    tory model of drug
    use, 67
Preble, Edward, 70
Pregnancy, smoking during,
    42
Prescription drugs, 65–66

Qingong, 89
Quintero, Gilbert, 29, 45,
    65–66

Recovery
    Alcoholics Anonymous
        program, 79–85
    changing the context of,
        92–93
    current treatment mod-
        els, 77
    efficacy in healing and,
        77–78
    ethnographic methods
        in drug treatment
        outcome studies,
        93–94
    increasing cultural con-
        gruence of treat-
        ments/prevention,
        90–92
    language of, 76
    mutual help models of,
        79–85
    understanding why
        treatments do not
        diffuse, 85–87
    utilizing indigenous cul-
        ture in, 87–89
Rogers, Everett M., 37, 85

Schonberg, Jeff, 2, 3, 69, 70
Sexton, Rocky, 64
Shafer, K. C., 86
Shaw, Susan, 70, 71
Singer, Merrill, 7, 53, 56,
    58, 60, 62, 69–70, 72,
    76
Skorpen, A., 42
Smith, Frederick, 3
Smith, P., 71

Smoking. *See* Cigarettes; Tobacco
Smoking cessation, grassroots counter-marketing billboard campaigns, 90–92
Spicer, R., 24
Spradley, James, 7–8, 28
Sterk, Claire, 63, 67–68
Stimulants, 65
Stimulants, definition of, 9
Stromberg, Peter, 46
Substance abuse/dependence, as diagnostic/culturally constructed terms, 5
Substance use
demonizing/romanticizing, 13
disorders, classification systems of, 12
Substance use/misuse, definition of, 5
Swora, Maria G., 84, 85

Tobacco
adolescents and smoking, 43–46
beliefs about smoking, 41
camaraderie and smoking, 41–42
cigarette marketing strategies, 46–49

diffusion of, 37–38
ethnographic studies of, 5–8
gender and smoking, 42–43
health consequences of, 39
indigenous uses of, 35–37
legal status of, 10–11
physiological effects of, 8–10
smoking bans, unintended consequences of, 49
See also Cigarettes
Tobacco companies
advertising to LGBT community, 48
antismoking advertising by, 47
Treatment
culturally sensitive, 92–93
definition of, 76
ethnographic research on methods of, 93–94
increasing cultural congruence of, 90–92
scientific research on efficacy of, 77–78
understanding cultural context of, 85–87

Trevor, William, 26
Trinh, T. H., 43

US Controlled Substances Act of 1970, 55

Volkow, Nora, 65
von Gernet, Alexander, 36

Waldram, James, 87, 88, 89
Warner, L., 10
Waterston, Alisse, 3, 4
Wechsler, Henry, 30
Weeks, M., 72
Wellin, E., 85
White, William, 76
Winter, Joseph, 9
Winter, Michael, 39
Women
crack cocaine use among, 67
drinking in Mayan Community, 20
link between smoking and camaraderie in, 42, 49
smoking among, 42–43
Women for Sobriety, 82–83

Zerger, Suzanne, 48
Ziker, John, 23, 24, 25
Zywiak, William, 40, 92

About the Author

Irene Glasser is an anthropologist whose work includes homelessness and addictions. She is the author of *More Than Bread: Ethnography of a Soup Kitchen*, *Homelessness in Global Perspective*, and *Braving the Street: The Anthropology of Homelessness* (coauthored with Rae Bridgman). Glasser is a Research Associate in the Center for Alcohol and Addiction Studies, Brown University; Professor Emerita, Eastern Connecticut State University; and currently teaches anthropology at Roger Williams University.